A Guide to Early Photographic Processes

This book has been supported by the Associates of the V&A

A GUIDE TO EARLY PHOTOGRAPHIC PROCESSES

Brian Coe
Mark Haworth-Booth

VICTORIA
& ALBERT
MUSEUM

Considerable care has been taken with the preparation of the photographic images in this book to achieve faithful reproduction of the originals. Early photographs encompass an extremely wide range of surface, detail and finish with subtle variations in colour, tonal values and contrast. To ensure the retention of these qualities in reproduction a sensitive combination of duotone, tri-colour and four-colour processes has been employed entailing the use of sixteen different coloured inks and combinations of up to five different screen structures. The images are printed offset photo-lithography on high quality cartridge paper with a non-reflective coating. The most important factor in obtaining this level of reproduction has been the ability of the printer to work directly from the original material in almost every case.

FRONT COVER *Baron de Meyer, Tamara Karsavina, About 1908, Autochrome (see page 106)*
BACK COVER *Eva Watson-Schütze, Woman admiring a print, About 1910, Bromoil (see page 107)*

This publication has been devised by Brian Coe and Mark Haworth-Booth. Brian Coe contributes the Introduction, Key, Glossary and Chart. The Commentary is by Brian Coe and Mark Haworth-Booth, who also provides the bibliography.

High magnification photographs by Martin Wood, Kodak Museum

Published by The Victoria and Albert Museum in association with Hurtwood Press

Hardback (Hurtwood Press) ISBN 0 903696 23 1
Softback (Victoria and Albert Museum) ISBN 0 905209 40 0

Designed by Roger Huggett and Sharon Ellis Davies/Sinc
Printed in England by The Westerham Press

CONTENTS

FOREWORD

Roy Strong
Director, Victoria and Albert Museum

The national collection of the art of photography at the Victoria and Albert Museum is shown in changing displays in four galleries and members of the public can also see photographs by visiting the Print Room. This book inaugurates the new galleries. It has three purposes. Firstly, to provide a guide to the recognition of the major photographic processes from the period 1840–1914. Secondly, to illustrate the finest examples of each process. Thirdly, to give guidance as to the proper treatment of photographs in the home, small collection or archive.

One of the functions the Museum carries out is to give advice. For years visitors have brought photographs to the Print Room to receive guidance about process, date and authorship. As old processes, overtaken by technology, vanish into history the language of earlier times falls into obscurity. 'Calotype', 'salted paper print', 'albumen', 'collodion positive', 'platinotype' – to say nothing of 'Bromoil' and 'gum bichromate' – do not trip readily from the tongue. No doubt the most plentiful kind of modern photograph, the so-called 'chromogenic' colour snap, will one day become haltingly discerned material from remote times. The black and white gelatin-silver print of our time arrives at the end of this book. One of the Museum's purposes, therefore, is to help the general public to become reacquainted with the outline and aspect of historical types of photograph: to offer a directory to the history of photographic processes, preferably seen at their very best.

From the experience of the past decade and a half I feel sure that much of the history of photography remains in obscurity, waiting to be recognised, studied and, very likely, properly conserved and maintained. This publication may help such discoveries to be made. I recall that a brief radio interview I gave on the art of photography led within a few hours to an individual bringing to the Museum's Print Room a set of Francis Frith's brilliant photographs of the Pyramids from the 1850s. The portfolio had been heroically supporting one leg of an imperfect kitchen table somewhere in London. Mark Haworth-Booth, the Assistant Keeper of Photographs, has a host of similar stories. The book, therefore, contains illustrations of the major processes; a commentary on the plates; an identification key; a chart indicating the periods at which processes flourished; and notes on the care of photographs.

The book and exhibition have been devised by Mark Haworth-Booth, and the Curator of the Kodak Museum, Brian Coe. For some years now Brian Coe has given one-day seminars on the recognition of photographic processes. His courses are designed for the many archivists and curators who have suddenly woken up to the variety and value of the photographs in their care. This sort of recognition is occurring in institutions all over the country – indeed in many parts of the world – and among the public at large. This inaugural book, and the exhibition accompanying it, projects Brian Coe's key – many years in the making – in a way that will be of benefit not only to professional colleagues but to the amateur enthusiast. It is an open seminar conducted by a very able and much admired colleague who kindly set aside the time to work with our own staff. The Museum's conservator of photographs, Elizabeth Martin, has provided the helpful notes on caring for photographs in the home, small collection or archive. We gratefully acknowledge the generosity of colleagues in helping to produce the book and exhibition, notably the Kodak Museum; Dr David Thomas and John Ward of the Science Museum, London; Kenneth Warr and Pamela Roberts of the Royal Photographic Society; and Dr Duncan Thomson and Sara Stevenson of the Scottish National Portrait Gallery, Edinburgh. The book and exhibition owe much, as always, to the enthusiastic support of Dr Michael Kauffmann, Keeper of Prints and Drawings and Photographs. This inaugural exhibition and publication have been generously supported by Ilford Ltd to whom the Museum is most grateful.

THE IDENTIFICATION OF EARLY PHOTOGRAPHS

The accurate identification of the various processes by which early photographs were made is not always easy. Many processes required that the photographer make his own materials, and the consequent variations due to imperfect chemicals and techniques, personal modifications of the process, and, in some instances, deterioration with the passage of time, make the task more difficult. Many processes existed in a number of variations, and prints made by one method may resemble closely those made by another. Nonetheless, in many instances the process may be identified, and the key that follows should help at least to narrow the range of possibilities.

The key covers only those processes in general use before the First World War. Colour photographs are not included. In attempting to identify a photograph, it is important to establish firstly that it is a true photograph and not a photo-mechanical reproduction, printed in ink from a plate or block. Often this is readily apparent; the picture may be printed on a book page or it may have a printer's credit below. To be sure, examine the print closely with the aid of a powerful magnifying glass – say ×10. Half-tone or letterpress printing of the type in use from the 1880s is easily identified. Under the lens, or even to the naked eye, the image can be seen to be made up of regular dots of differing sizes, or, sometimes, of lines of varying thickness. Generally, the quality of the reproduction lacks the subtle gradations of a true photograph. Some reproductions have more of the character of a photograph; examination with the lens may reveal an irregular but well defined reticulated or grained structure, indicating that it was made by one of the many variations of the collotype printing process, widely used from the 1870s for quality reproductions. Good examples, printed in a suitable ink colour, and sometimes varnished, may at first sight seem to be real photographs. The photomechanical process whose prints are most likely to be confused with real photographs is photogravure, in general use from the 1880s. The prints were often made from plates grained with a fine powder, and under a lens the print may show a grainy appearance, rather different from that seen in a much enlarged photograph. The photogravure image will not normally show a well-defined, regular structure. Such prints are generally easily identified by the printer's credit often given below the picture, and the impression in the paper of the printing plate – the plate mark. Photogravure printing was used for the quality reproduction of the work of some pictorial photographers in the 1890s and 1900s. The prints could be tipped into publications, from which they may become detached, or could be distributed 'loose', printed on thin card, or in 'window' mounts, often printed on thin, even tissue papers. Even in the absence of printer's credits and the

FIG. 1 *Photomechanical print processes.* A *Halftone print and detail. Note the regular dot pattern.* B *Collotype print and detail. The reticulated structure of the image is very characteristic.* C *Photogravure print and detail. The granular structure of the image is rather more pronounced than that of an ordinary photograph.*

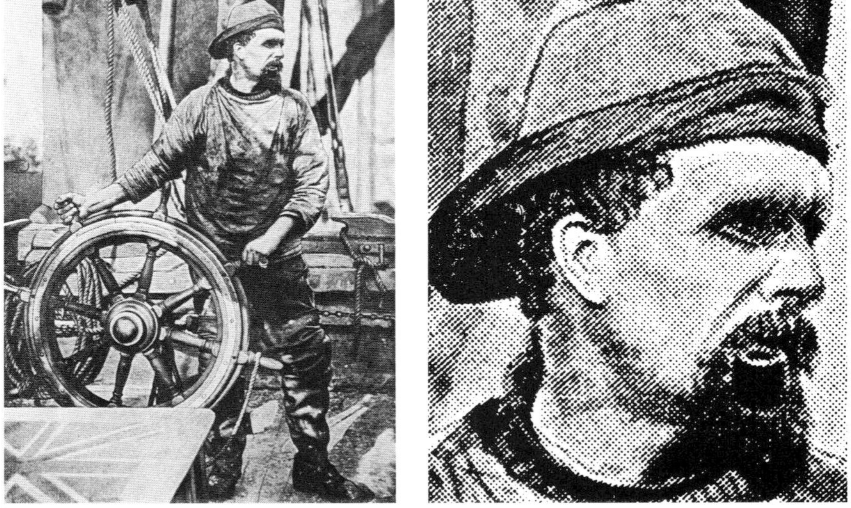

A

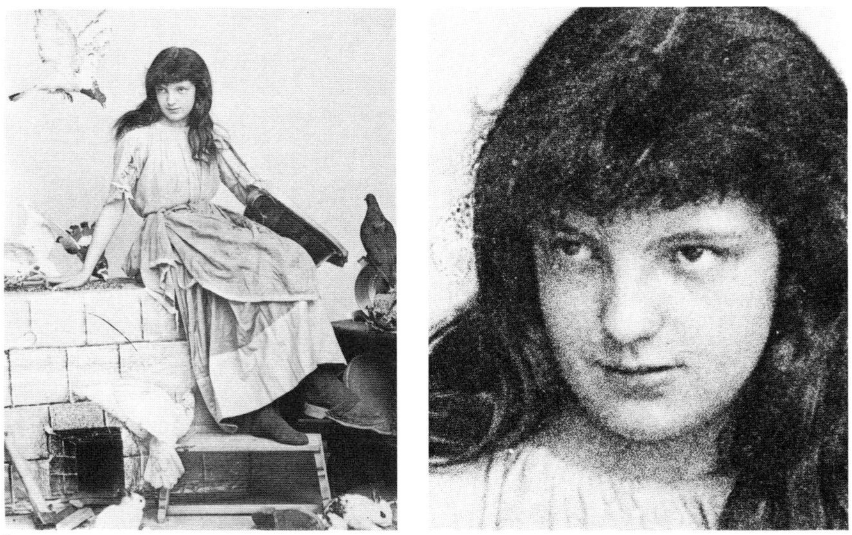

B

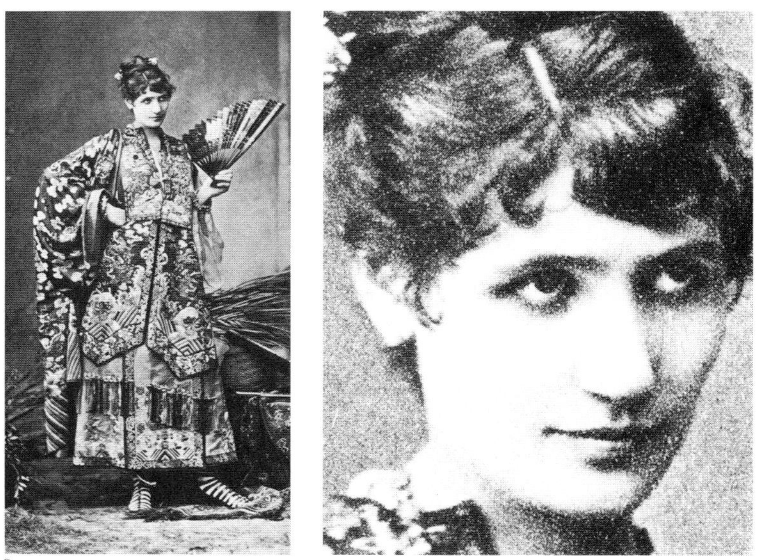

C

like, the 'ink-on-paper' nature of the image, and its soft-grained structure, will generally be apparent enough to distinguish the photogravure from the true photograph.

At each step in the key that follows you are presented with two or more choices. Consider each one carefully, choose one, and move on to the numbered step indicated until you reach a name. A fuller description of each process will be found in the glossary following the key. Remember, some of these processes may be distinguished only by very subtle differences. A powerful lens, at least $\times 10$, is desirable, so that the fine structure of the image and of the paper surface can be examined. Reference will be made to coated and uncoated papers. The latter are found in processes in which the light-sensitive chemicals are formed within the paper structure; such papers will have the surface appearance of ordinary, plain writing or drawing paper, although occasionally rougher papers will be met with. Coated papers carry the light-sensitive material in a coating on the surface of the paper. This layer may be very thin, detectable only by the sheen it imparts to the surface; if the print is unmounted, the front and back surfaces may be compared for texture and highlight colour. It may be, as in the case of modern materials, a thick layer completely masking the paper surface. If the print is unmounted, a useful clue is given by the tendency of most coated papers to curl towards the image side when dry, while uncoated papers normally remain flat. Although coated papers may be easy to distinguish when the coating is glossy, when it is matt, as in the gelatin papers especially popular at the turn of the century, the difference may be hard to see. A matt coated paper has a lifeless quality, especially apparent in the darker areas. Plain paper is never totally lacking in 'life'. Carbon prints made on rough paper may also be matt, but usually show some slight glossiness in the dark areas. It is worth pointing out that most of the processes covered by the key gave prints that could be, and frequently were, hand-coloured in oils or water-colours, sometimes to the extent of almost entirely hiding the photographic image, which may be glimpsed at unpainted edges.

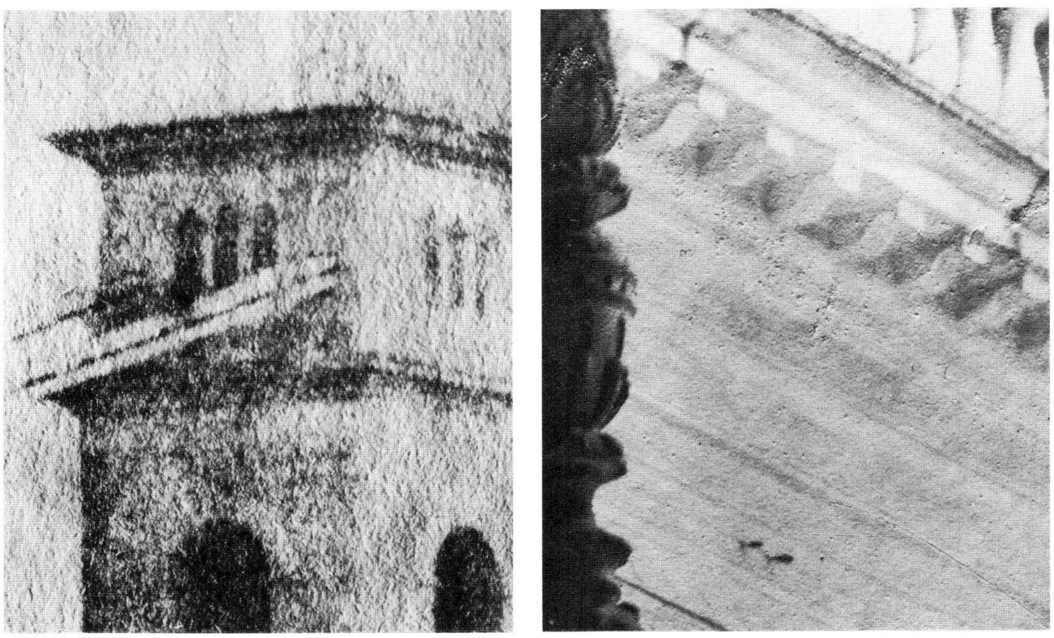

A B

FIG. 2 *A comparison of plain and coated paper surfaces, enlarged.* A *Salted paper print, in which the image is carried within the fibrous paper structure.* B *Gelatin coated paper, with a smooth coating on the surface in which the image is formed.*

The nomenclature of early processes to some extent has become confused in recent years by the misuse of some terms. The description 'silver print' should be used only to distinguish between those processes in which the image is of silver and those in which it is a pigment, or some other metal. To use it alone to describe prints made on gelatin based papers is misleading. Gelatin-silver print is the preferred usage. Collodion positive photographs are often called Ambrotypes; strictly, this should be applied only to collodion positives prepared by a patented variant of the process, operated in America in the 1850s, although popular misusage from the 1850s onwards has perhaps by now legitimised its use. The term 'salted paper print' is preferable to the less precise 'salt print'. A calotype print is a salted paper print made from a paper negative; salted paper prints from glass negatives should not be called calotypes. The description 'albumenised salt print' is sometimes used to describe a lightly albumenised print. Since the only difference between a salted paper print and an albumen print is the presence of the albumen, such a description should not be used. The print is either a salted paper print *or* an albumen print – not both! Contrary to widespread belief the name Daguerreotype refers not to any photograph in a case, but to certain such photographs made by the process introduced by L.J.M. Daguerre in 1839. The term 'sepia' is often used as a blanket description for all prints without black and white tones. The true sepia colour is a yellower brown than the reddish or purplish browns found in many early prints. Toned gelatin-silver prints are often of a true sepia colour. In the key that follows the various shades of brown are described, but the reader should refer to the colour illustrations for further guidance. 'Emulsion' is used frequently to cover all forms of light-sensitive coating on papers or negatives. The only processes for which this is accurate are those based on gelatin, in which a suspension, or emulsion, of silver salts is made in liquid gelatin and then coated on the base. The term should not be used for albumen papers, collodion plates or salted papers and so on, where no emulsion is formed.

KEY TO THE IDENTIFICATION OF PROCESSES

1 Negative image → *2*.
Positive image → *11*.

2 Negative on transparent base → *3*.
Negative on paper → *8*.

3 Negative on glass → *4*.
Negative on flexible film → *5*.

4 Hold the plate against a black surface and observe the colour of the reflected image (FIG 15).
Image creamy or milky in colour; coating on plate may be uneven at the edges and corners.
ALBUMEN *or* COLLODION NEGATIVE
or Image dark by reflection (discount shiny tarnishing found on some old negatives), coating on plate even to the edges.
GELATIN DRY PLATE

5 Film highly inflammable (test with small shaving cut from the edge) → *6*.
Film burns with difficulty, or slowly, or not at all → *7*.

6 Thin film, tending to curl into a tight roll.
NITRATE ROLLFILM
or Thin film, tending to remain flat, or nearly so.
NITRATE ROLL FILM, NON-CURL
or Film medium thick, flat, may show residual emulsion in a strip along one edge.
FILM-PACK NEGATIVE
or Film medium thick to thick, may show manufacturer's name or edge notching code.
NITRATE SHEET FILM NEGATIVE

7 Film thin.
SAFETY ROLL FILM
or Film medium thick to thick, may show manufacturer's name, edge notching codes and be stamped 'Safety'.
SHEET FILM NEGATIVE
or Film very thick, perhaps brittle.
INSOLUBLE GELATIN SHEET FILM

8 Negative on plain paper, relatively opaque → *9*.
Negative on translucent paper → *10*.

9 Negative on uncoated writing or drawing paper; image formed within the paper; size usually larger than 100 × 125 mm.
CALOTYPE NEGATIVE
or Negative on coated paper, often less than 100 × 125 mm.
PAPER NEGATIVE
or Negative on thin coated card.
PAPER NEGATIVE FOR REFLECTION PRINTING

10 Paper waxed, usually larger than 100 × 125 mm. Waxed negatives usually show white creases or stress marks.
WAXED PAPER NEGATIVE PROCESS *or*
CALOTYPE NEGATIVE, WAXED
or Paper oiled, may be quite yellow; usually smaller than 100 × 125 mm.
EASTMAN NEGATIVE PAPER

11 Positive print on paper or card → *12*.
Positive print on other materials → *18*.

12 Image formed within uncoated paper (FIG 4) → *13*.
Image carried in a coating on paper surface (FIG 4) → *14*.

13 Image reddish-brown, may verge on purplish-brown, but often may be partly or wholly faded to yellow especially at edges. Highlights white – the colour of the paper base.
SALTED PAPER PRINT
or Image black and white, or nearly so, highlights usually white – the colour of the paper base. May show some fading to yellow, especially at edges.
BLANQUART-EVRARD PROCESS
(*Developed salted paper print*)
or Image black and white, with silvery-grey ones and rich blacks or warm brown; wide tonal range. No sign of fading or tarnishing of image, although darkest blacks very occasionally may show a trace of metallic 'bronzing'.
PLATINUM PRINT, PLATINOTYPE
or Image Prussian Blue colour
CYANOTYPE *or* BLUEPRINT
or Image may be of almost any colour, often on rough paper. Pigment image, usually lacking in fine detail and with broad tonal effects. Often resembles crayon or charcoal drawings.
GUM BICHROMATE PRINT
or Image in pigment on thin or tissue paper; image colour usually but not invariably black. No sign of fading or tarnishing. Limited resolution of detail and broad tonal effects.
OIL PIGMENT TRANSFER PRINT

14 Image black and white, neutral tones → *16*.
Image not black and white → *15*.

15 Light to medium coating on thin paper, giving anything from a light sheen to a distinct gloss to the surface. Image reddish-brown, often partially faded to yellow, especially at edges, and the highlights more or less yellowed. When gold toning has been used, the image colour will be rich purplish-brown, and the highlights will be white, or almost neutral in colour. The paper base may be tinted pink or pale purple (from 1860s) to counteract effect of yellowed highlights.

ALBUMEN PAPER PRINT

or Medium to thick coating, usually glossy or smooth, on medium thick paper or thin card. Image colours range from reddish-brown to purplish-brown. Highlights usually white, or nearly so.

PRINTING-OUT PAPER PRINT

or Medium to thick coating, may be glossy, semi-matt, matt or textured. Image sepia, or sometimes other colours e.g. green, blue, etc. Highlights white, except when paper base is cream or ivory tinted. Paper base medium thick to thick, or card.

GELATIN-SILVER PRINT, DEVELOPED AND TONED

or Medium coating, surface usually smooth – 'eggshell' finish, but on rough paper may take up texture of paper surface although the darkest areas may show more gloss. Pigment image, no fading or tarnishing → *17*.

16 Medium to thick coating, may be matt, semi-matt, glossy or textured. Image black and white, may show some fading, or more usually, metallic tarnishing of darker tones, especially at the edges.
Paper base medium thick to thick, or card; white, ivory or cream.

GELATIN-SILVER PRINT, DEVELOPED

or Medium coating, surface usually smooth – 'eggshell' finish, but on rough paper may take up texture of paper surface although darkest areas may show more gloss. Pigment image, no fading or tarnishing → *17*.

17 Print often mounted on book page or printed card; may be marked 'Permanent' or 'Autotype'. Image colour usually brown or black and white, but may be any other colour. The image may show distinct relief – contours visible at boundaries between dark and light areas (FIG 6).

CARBON PRINT

or Print always mounted on book page or printed card, usually named on the mount 'Woodburytype' or 'Photoglyptie'. Image colour usually, but not invariably, chocolate brown, and may show pronounced relief.

WOODBURYTYPE PRINT

or Image in pigment, often but not invariably black. Broad tonal effects and limited resolution of detail.

OIL PIGMENT *or* BROMOIL PRINT

18 Positive on metal → *19*.
Positive on other materials → *22*.

19 Image on highly-polished silver-suraced copper plate, usually in a case or frame. The image may appear as a negative or a positive, depending on the reflection of a white or dark background (FIG 9).

DAGUERREOTYPE

or Image on other metal → *20*.

20 Positive image on black or chocolate-brown enamelled tinplate – readily attracted to a magnet. May show signs of rusting on front or back. May be loose, framed or cased, or mounted in card.

FERROTYPE *or* TINTYPE

or Positive on other metal → *21*.

21 Black and white or toned silver image transferred to metal sheet.

TRANSFEROTYPE PRINT

or Brown or other color pigment image transferred to metal sheet.

CARBON TRANSFER PRINT

or Image on metal-coated paper, black and white or toned silver image.

METOTYPE PRINT *or* METALOTYPE

22 Positive on glass → *23*.
Positive on other materials → *28*.

23 Transparent positive, normally viewed by transmitted light → *24*.
Opaque positive, normally viewed by reflected light → *26*.

24 Place transparency on a black surface.
Image creamy by reflection, showing as negative; may be cold, even bluish-black, by transmitted light. Usually stereoscopic transparency or lantern slide.

COLLODION *or* ALBUMEN TRANSPARENCY

or Image dark by reflection (discount any metallic tarnishing) → *25*.

25 Image black and white (but may show some fading or tarnishing) or sepia, or may be toned in other colours.

GELATIN-SILVER TRANSPARENCY

or Image usually chocolate brown, but may be in other colours. May show strong relief image – contours between dark and light areas. No sign of fading or tarnishing.

CARBON TRANSFER PRINT *or*
WOODBURYTYPE TRANSPARENCY

26 Negative image on glass, which backed with black paint appears as a positive paper or cloth. Image creamy or silvery by reflection.
Usually in case or frame.

COLLODION POSITIVE

or Image on white opal glass → *27*.
Albumen print stuck on rear of curved glass, coloured on rear.

CRYSTOLEUM PRINT

or Gelatin print stuck on rear of thick, flat, bevelled glass, usually gilt-edged.

OPALINE PRINT

27 Silver image on opal glass – may show tarnishing or fading, especially at edges. Image usually black and white, frequently hand-coloured.
OPALOTYPE *or* OPAL PRINT

or Pigment image transferred to opal glass, no fading or tarnishing of image; image colour usually black and white or sepia, often hand coloured. Irregular edge of the transferred image may be visible towards the edge of the plate.
OPALOTYPE *or* OPAL PRINT *(Carbon transfer print)*

28 Image on ceramic, glassware, or enamel, fired in the glaze.
PHOTOCERAMIC

or Picture, on surface only, on ceramic, glass or enamel.
CARBON TRANSFER PRINT *or* TRANSFEROTYPE

or Picture on other materials → *29*.

29 Image on black leather (real, synthetic or oilcloth), image whitish or creamy.
COLLODION POSITIVE

or Image on white or light leather, image black and white or sepia.
CARBON TRANSFER PRINT

or Image formed in fabric; various image colours.
FABRIC PRINT: PLATINOTYPE, CYANOTYPE *or* SALTED PAPER PRINT PROCESS

or Image on coated fabric, generally gelatin silver.
FABRIC PRINT: PRINT ON PROPRIETARY COATED LINEN

or Image on wood, stone, mother-of-pearl etc.
CARBON TRANSFER PRINT *or* TRANSFEROTYPE PRINT

or Image on synthetic ivory.
EBURNEUM PRINT

or Image on white or coloured opaque celluloid.
GELATIN PRINT

NOTE

Photographs made in the 1850s and early 1860s may have been made either from glass plate negatives, by the wet collodion or albumen processes, or from paper negatives, generally of the waxed-paper variety. Since the latter process was capable of recording quite fine detail, it may not be immediately evident from the print which type of negative had been used, especially since both albumen and plain salted papers were used to print from both glass and paper negatives, at least in the early 1850s. Clues may be found if the print is closely inspected, preferably using a magnifier (FIG 17).

Prints from paper negatives will show some breaking-up or mottling of the image due to the fibrous structure of the negative. This will be most evident in areas of even medium density and on the edges of details in the image. The print may show an inscription printed from the negative; in the case of a paper negative, which could be written on in ink, the inscription will always appear in white. The collodion surface took ink less readily, and it was usual to scratch the inscription with a needle point (FIG 3). The print will show this as black but note that inscriptions in white are regularly found. The often irregular edge to the collodion coating may show on the print in the form of black corners or patches at the edges of the picture.

Coating defects appearing as well defined spots or other marks in the print may have been present in the original collodion negative; defects on paper negatives are rarely well-defined. If the edge of the negative appears in a print, the presence of a well-defined thin white line at the very edge between the border and the image will indicate that a transparent negative was used; prints from paper negatives will show no such white line, or at least an ill-defined one.

FORMATS

Since the introduction of photography in 1839 there have been a large number of negative sizes and size alone is no infallible guide to age. The first Daguerreotype camera was designed for plates $6\frac{1}{2} \times 8\frac{1}{2}$ inches (216×165 mm) and this became the whole-plate size. Various subdivisions of this were used, of which the half-plate, $4\frac{3}{4} \times 6\frac{1}{2}$ inches (120×165 mm) and quarter-plate, $3\frac{1}{4} \times 4\frac{1}{4}$ inches (88×108 mm) were the most popular for general photography, up to comparatively recently. Many larger and smaller sizes, some based on Imperial measurements, others on metric, were used over the years. Until towards the end of the last century, the vast majority of prints were made by contact printing, giving a print the same size as the negative. Larger format negatives were therefore more likely to be used, especially for landscape and architectural photography. The advent of enlargers and enlarging papers led progressively to reductions in negative sizes which culminated in the use today of mostly small formats.

The introduction of roll film cameras in the late 1880s led to the appearance of a number of new formats, most of them smaller than the contemporary glass plate sizes. For roll film negatives, or uncropped prints from them, the size of the negative may give a clue as to the earliest possible date.

$2\frac{1}{2}$ inch (63·5 mm) *from* The Kodak Camera, introduced 1888
$3\frac{1}{2}$ inch (89 mm) circular *from* No 2 Kodak camera, 1889
$1\frac{1}{2} \times 2$ inches (38 × 50 mm) *from* Pocket Kodak camera, 1895
$2\frac{1}{4} \times 2\frac{1}{4}$ inches (57 × 57 mm) *from* No 1 Brownie camera, 1900
$2\frac{1}{4} \times 3\frac{1}{4}$ inches (57 × 82·5 mm) *from* Folding Pocket Kodak camera, 18
$3\frac{1}{4} \times 5\frac{1}{2}$ inches (82·5 × 139·7 mm) *from* No 3A Folding Pocket Kodak camera, 1903
$3\frac{1}{2} \times 12$ inches (89 × 305 mm) *from* No 4 Panoram Kodak camera, 1899
$2\frac{1}{4} \times 7$ inches (57 × 178 mm) *from* No 1 Panoram Kodak camera, 1900
$1\frac{5}{8} \times 2\frac{1}{2}$ inches (41·3 × 63·5 mm) *from* Vest Pocket Kodak camera, 1912
$1\frac{1}{2} \times 2\frac{1}{4}$ inches (38·1 × 57 mm) *from* Ensignette camera, 1909
2 × 3 inches (50·8 × 76·2 mm) *from* No 2 Ensignette camera, 1909

There were many other roll film negative sizes, but most were the same as plate sizes in general use, and therefore they are of less help in dating. Most of the larger roll film sizes did not survive long after the Second World War.

In the last century, photographic prints were sold in various forms. Daguerreotypes and collodion positives, and some paper prints, were supplied in protective cases or frames. Unmounted prints could be bought from photographers and printsellers, and were usually pasted into albums by the owner. From around 1860, the *carte de visite* photograph became very popular. It took the form of a print mounted on a thick card approximately $2\frac{1}{2} \times 4\frac{1}{8}$ inches (63·5 × 10·5 mm) in size, usually printed, often elaborately, on the back with the photographer's name and address. The carte remained in general use until the turn of the century. A similar mounted print, the Cabinet, in a larger size of approximately $4\frac{1}{4} \times 6\frac{1}{2}$ inches (108 × 165 mm) was introduced in 1866 and survived until the First World War, by which time it had become the usual practice to supply commercial portraits in folders or slip-in mounts rather than mounted on thick cards.

The stereoscopic photograph was popularised at the 1851 Great Exhibition, and for many years after the collection and viewing of stereoscopic photographs was something of a craze.

The stereoscopic photograph mount was approximately $3\frac{1}{2} \times 7$ inches (89 × 178 mm) bearing two similar photographs representing left eye and right eye views of the scenes, which combined to give an image in full depth and relief when seen in a special viewer. Almost all the principal photographic processes were used at one time or another for stereoscopic work. Stereoscopic photography saw some decline in interest after the 1860s, but underwent a revival in the 1890s and 1900s, with the appearance of snapshot cameras with which the amateur could take his or her own stereoscopic pictures.

The magic lantern slide could be produced photographically. The earliest photographic slides date from 1849, when albumen transparencies on glass were made for projection. The collodion and gelatin-silver processes were also used for slide making. The majority of lantern slides normally encountered are from the 1890s and later, when more manageable and efficient light sources made the use of the lantern in the home more practical. The standard British lantern slide size is $3\frac{1}{4} \times 3\frac{1}{4}$ inches (82·5 × 82·5 mm); Continental and American slides are $3\frac{1}{4} \times 4$ inches (82·5 × 102 mm).

The rise in popularity of the picture postcard led to the appearance from around 1902 of sensitised cards with gelatin-silver emulsions one side and the other side printed for the address and inscription, with a central dividing line.

Several popular snapshot cameras appeared taking postcard sized negatives – $3\frac{1}{4} \times 5\frac{1}{2}$ inches (82·5 × 140 mm,), and professional photographers would supply portraits in this format for easy transmission to friends or relatives.

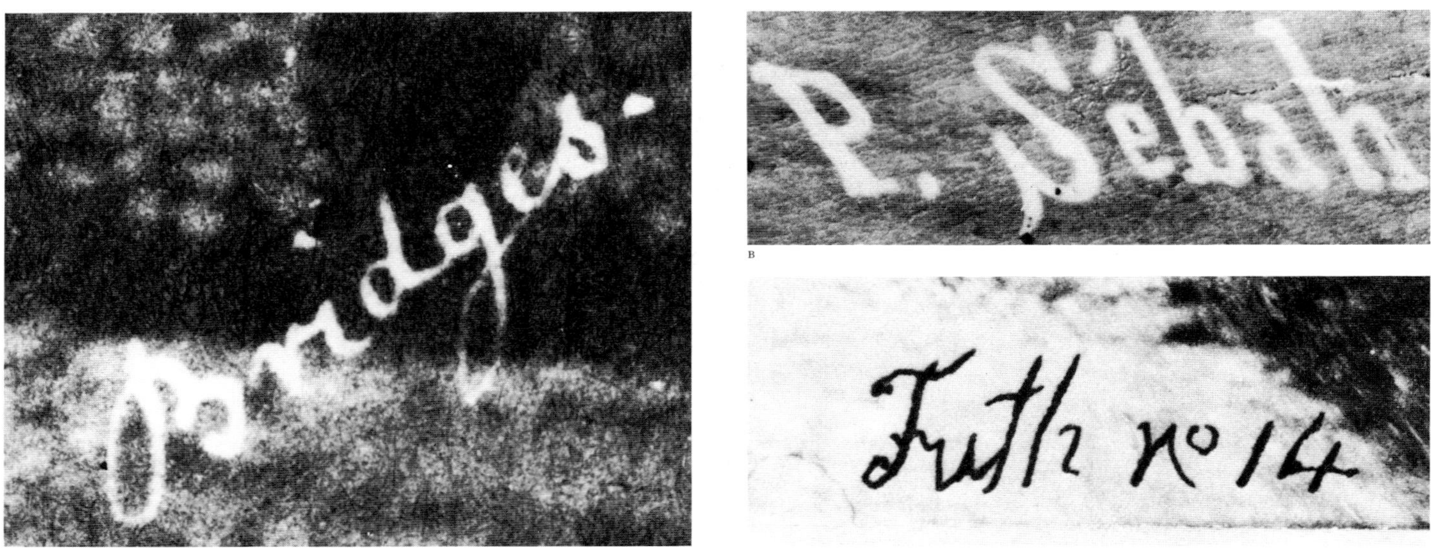

A B C

FIG. 3 *Inscriptions on negatives.* A *On prints from paper negatives, inscriptions and signatures will always appear in white.* B *On prints from glass negatives, inscriptions may be in white, but will show better resolution.* C *Inscriptions in black, produced by scratching through the collodion or gelatin coating, can only be printed from glass negatives.*

GLOSSARY

Albumen Paper Prints *1850 to c1900*
This process was introduced by L.D. Blanquart-Evrard and remained the principal medium for photographic printing until the end of the century, when it was superseded by the gelatin based papers. Essentially an improvement on the salted paper process (q.v.), it used thin plain paper coated with a layer of egg-white containing salt (FIG 4). The coating could vary from the merest film, giving a just perceptible sheen to the paper (mostly found in early prints) to an appreciably thick, almost glossy, coating (FIG 5). The albumenised paper was sensitised with silver nitrate solution before use. Printing was done by daylight under a negative, printing times ranging from many minutes to hours for each print. The fixed albumen print had a reddish-brown image colour; residual silver compounds in the albumen reacted with sulphur compounds in the atmosphere to produce a yellow stain in the whites, or highlights, of the print usually within a relatively short time after printing. This yellowing provides a useful means of distinguishing a lightly coated albumen print, of the sort common in the 1850s, from a salted paper print, whose whites would normally be clean. From 1863, albumen papers with pink or purple tinted bases were sold to help counteract the yellowing effect. Albumen prints could be toned with a gold solution. This imparted a rich purplish-brown colour to the image, and if properly carried out, protected the whites from yellowing and reduced the risk of fading the image.

Albumen Negatives *1848 to 1860s*
The use of a film of sensitised albumen on glass was first proposed by Abel Niépce de Saint-Victor; the process was used to some extent for a few years for landscape and architectural photography and the like. The albumen plate gave very high resolution of detail but was very slow, requiring long exposures. In the 1850s it was employed in combination with collodion or gelatin in the preparation of dry plates. Albumen negatives are not commonly met with, and in any case, are almost impossible to distinguish from collodion negatives, at least not without complex chemical tests.

Albumen Transparencies *1849 to c1914*
Albumen coated glass plates were used by the Langenheim brothers in America under the name Hyalotypes for lantern-slide making from 1849. The process was taken up in the 1850s for the production of stereoscopic transparencies, notably by Ferrier and Soulier. It remained in use up to the First World War for the commercial production of lantern slides (FIG 14).

Blanquart-Evrard Process *1851 to c1857*
L.D. Blanquart-Evrard introduced a process for the development of salted paper prints (q.v.) at his studio in Lille in 1851. The sensitised salted paper was exposed under a negative to daylight for only a few seconds, and was then developed. Several hundred prints a day could be made from one negative, instead of the handful possible by the normal printing-out process. Large runs of prints were made for book illustrations and print editions. Thomas Sutton also operated the process from his studio in Jersey in 1855 and 1856.

Developed salted paper prints show the characteristic effect of an image in the paper (FIG 17), but the image colour is a neutral or near neutral black and white, quite unlike the reddish tones of the printed-out paper; the highlights may be appreciably yellowed in some prints. The usual presence of some image deterioration, at least at the edges, and the 1850s context of the photographs should distinguish these prints from the much later platinum prints (q.v.)

Bromoil Prints *1907 to 1940s*
Developed by C. Welbourne Piper from an idea by E.J. Wall, it was a variant of the oil-pigment process (q.v.). Prints, or more usually, enlargements were made on a suitable gelatin-silver bromide paper, and the image was bleached in a solution containing potassium bichromate. The gelatin became selectively hardened so that it would take up more or less pigment when hand applied with special brushes. The bleached image was thus 'redeveloped' in pigment, the distribution of which was to a large extent under the photographer's control. Bromoil prints, which may be in a variety of colours, generally show broader tonal effects and more diffuse detail than conventional prints.

Calotype Process *1840 to c1855*
The process was discovered by W.H.F. Talbot in 1840 and was patented by him in 1841. Fine quality writing paper was sensitised with potassium iodide and silver nitrate solutions and exposed in the camera, typically from ten to sixty seconds in sunlight. The negative was then developed in a solution of gallic acid and silver nitrate, and fixed. The paper was generally waxed after processing to make it translucent, and was printed in sunlight onto salted paper (q.v.). The process was popular with amateur photographers, mainly for landscape and architec-

tural work, until the 1850s when it was superseded by the waxed paper process (q.v.) and the wet collodion process (q.v.). Calotype prints are capable of showing quite fine detail, but can be identified by the characteristic mottling produced by the paper fibres in the negative, most easily seen in areas of even, mid tones or at the edges between dark and light areas (a powerful lens may be needed).

CARBON PROCESS *c1860 to 1930s*
Early forms of this widely used process were invented by A.L. Poitevin in 1855 and J. Pouncy in 1858, but the successful introduction of carbon printing followed improvements by J.W. Swan in 1864. A sheet of paper, the 'tissue', coated with gelatin containing a suitable pigment – sometimes carbon black, hence the name – together with potassium bichromate was exposed to daylight under a negative. The dense parts of the negative protected the carbon 'tissue' from light, and here the gelatin remained soluble; elsewhere, in proportion to exposure, the gelatin hardened. After exposure, the 'tissue' was washed with hot water to remove the more soluble gelatin and thus to 'develop' the image. Since the surface of the 'tissue' was made insoluble, it was normally transferred before development face down onto another support; the original paper base of the 'tissue' detached as the development proceeded. Prints produced this way were laterally reversed, left for right; this could be corrected by a second transfer to a final sheet, after development.

The relief image formed during the process can sometimes be seen on carbon prints, especially those produced by a single transfer (FIG 6). If present, the effect is most easily seen as a contour at the edge between a dark and a light area. Carbon images are permanent, and will show no sign of fading or deterioration. They were much in use for book illustration and commercial editions of photographs in the 1870s and 1880s. The carbon image could be transferred to practically any surface: glass, both clear and opal, ceramics, wood, leather, metal as well as all kinds of paper, both rough and smooth, and card.

COLLODIO-CHLORIDE PAPERS *see* GELATIN-SILVER PAPERS

COLLODION NEGATIVES *1851 to c1885*
The first fully practical process for negatives on glass was introduced by F. Scott Archer in 1851. A sheet of glass was hand-coated with a thin film of collodion (guncotton dissolved in ether) containing potassium iodide, and was sensitised on the spot with silver nitrate. The plate had to be exposed while still wet, and developed immediately. Collodion negatives gave a very high resolution of detail; exposure times normally ranged from some seconds to a minute or two depending on conditions. Dry collodion plates, made by covering the collodion with a layer of albumen or gelatin were introduced in 1855, and were commercially available from 1856, but they were much less sensitive than the wet process which remained popular until superseded by the gelatin dry plates (q.v.) introduced in the 1870s.

Collodion negatives have a characteristic milky or creamy look when seen against a black surface, reflecting a positive image. The coating is usually uneven at the edges and corners, at least one of which, held by the photographer during coating, may be quite free of coating. The collodion layer may show 'crazy-paving' cracks due to shrinkage (FIG 15). 'Comets' – coating defects in the form of a spot with a comet-like tail – may be present in the image, and can sometimes be seen in prints from collodion negatives. The 'shadows' of the diagonal silver wires on which the plate rested in the special plateholder may be visible across the corners of the negative – although plates by later processes exposed in earlier cameras may show the same effect.

COLLODION POSITIVES *1852 to c1890*
The suggestion that a 'thin', underexposed collodion negative (q.v.) might be backed with black to form a positive was made in 1852 by the process's inventor F. Scott Archer. It was in widespread use by the mid 1850s, and although becoming less popular after the introduction of the *carte de visite* photograph, around 1860, continued in use into the 1880s and even beyond, especially in small studios. The collodion positive, sometimes called an Ambrotype, from a variant of the process patented in America, used a collodion negative on glass painted black on the back, or mounted with a black cloth or paper backing. Usually the picture was mounted with a decorative mask or matt and a cover glass, fitted in a case or frame, like the Daguerreotype, (q.v.) with which it is sometimes confused. While the Daguerreotype image may show as a negative or as a positive depending on the reflections of a light or dark ground, regardless of the angle of view. The collodion positive always shows as a positive: its negative character can be seen only by transmitted light (FIG 7).

The process existed in several variants. Depending on the chemical treatment, the image colour can range from the normal creamy colour to a silvery white or even to a snow-white – a result known as Alabastrine. In the Relievo process introduced by Urie in 1854 and revived by T.C. Lawrence in 1857, the background to a portrait was scraped away, or the sitter was photographed against a dark background. White, coloured or painted backing papers were set behind the plate, which was painted black only behind the figure (FIG 8). The effect was one of the figure standing out from the background, from which it was separated by the thickness of the plate. The Ambrotype was a variant in which the cover-glass was sealed to the plate by Canada Balsam, an idea of James Cutting in 1854.

Another variant used black, or more usually deep red or purple glass, which removed the need to back the picture, and added a hint of colour to the image. Collodion positives were made on black leather in the 1850s – rendering them less likely to be damaged when posted in the mail. Occasionally, collodion positives are found made on a black waterproof coating on paper. The most common variant of the process is the Ferrotype (q.v.).

COLLODION TRANSPARENCIES *1850s to 1910s*
The collodion process could be used to make positive transparencies on glass, and was popular in this application long after it ceased to be used for negatives. Collodion transparencies show the characteristic creamy image when seen against a black surface; this time, however, the reflected image is seen as a negative (FIG 14).

COLLOTYPE PRINTING *early 1870s to date*
A photomechanical printing process in which a metal or glass

plate, coated with bichromated gelatin, was exposed under a negative. When the moistened gelatin dried, it reticulated, forming a fine-grained mesh-like structure on the surface, which took up greasy ink in proportion to the hardening produced by exposure. The ink was then transferred from the plate to paper, in a press. A number of processes based on this principle were in use, and it is still operated for short run quality printing. Collotype prints show a well defined, very characteristic irregular grain pattern when magnified.

CRYSTOLEUM *1880s to 1910s*
A print on thin paper, usually albumen, was stuck face down on the inside of a curved glass, and the paper was thinned down by sandpapering until it was almost removed. Colours were applied to the back of the print and to a white backing sheet which was bound up with it. The effect was of a finely coloured photograph with none of its details obscured by paint, as was normally the case. The process was a development of one used in the 18th century for colouring engravings.

CYANOTYPE *1842 to 1950s*
A process invented by Sir John Herschel. Paper impregnated with iron salts was exposed to daylight in contact with a negative, or a drawing on tracing paper, producing an image in insoluble Prussian Blue in the paper, which was fixed by simply washing in water. It was not much used until the 1880s, the 1890s and 1900s, when because of its simplicity the process became popular with amateurs for 'proofing' snapshot Negatives. Its principle use was for the copying of plans and drawings – hence the name 'blueprint' – which use continued almost to the present day. The process was used to illustrate the three volumes of *British Algae: Cyanotype Impressions* 1843–1853 by Mrs Anna Atkins.

DAGUERREOTYPE *1839 to c1860*
The first photographic process to be announced to the public, in 1839. A highly polished silver surface on a copper plate was sensitised by fumes from iodine, exposed in a camera, and the image developed by exposure to mercury vapour. At first the process was very insensitive, but optical and chemical improvements made portraiture possible, and from the early 1840s portrait studios opened in many cities and towns throughout the world.

The Daguerreotype image was easily damaged by touching, being on the surface of the silvered plate (FIG 10), and was protected in a case or frame, with a decorative mask or matt and a cover glass. Since the image is in the form of a greyish-white deposit on a shiny silver surface, the Daguerreotype has to be held so as to reflect a dark ground against which the image is seen as a positive. If the plate reflects a light ground, the image appears negative. This is unique to the process and is the most easily recognised feature when the Daguerreotype is in a case (FIG 9). Uncased plates will usually reveal the copper backing, although a proportion of plates, especially late examples, were made by electro-plating copper sheets, and will show a silver, but unpolished, surface on the back. Although normally sealed, the silver surface of the Daguerreotype may show iridescent tarnishing around the edges where airborne pollutants have reached the plate. Over-exposure of the plate in the camera produced 'solarisation' – the effect of which was to produce a bluish deposit in the whitest areas of the image, which may be mistaken for artificial colouring – which was indeed applied to a proportion of Daguerreotypes in any case.

EASTMAN NEGATIVE PAPER *see* PAPER NEGATIVES

EBURNEUM PRINTS *1865 to c1900*
A process invented by J.M. Burgess, in which a collodion or carbon transparency was backed by a mixture of gelatin and zinc oxide which set to give an ivory-like sheet which could be removed from the temporary support of waxed glass which had been used to carry the image. A similar effect was produced later by printing negatives on sheets of opaque white celluloid, sensitised with a gelatin-silver emulsion, and commercially available in the 1890s and 1900s.

FABRIC PRINTS
Photographic images may be made on any absorbent fabric such as linen, silk, canvas etc., by any of the processes used normally for sensitising plain paper. The platinum, cyanotype and salted paper processes (q.v.) were all used. Photogravure prints, usually on silk, were also made, especially around 1900. From the late 1890s, proprietary brands of gelatin-silver sensitised linen or linen-surfaced paper were available.

FERROTYPE *c1855 to 1930s*
The production of collodion positives (q.v.) on black enamelled tinplate was suggested by several workers in the early 1850s, but was not adopted on any scale until after the American patent for the process by Hamilton Smith in 1855; he called such pictures Melainotypes. Pictures on black, or from the late 1860s, chocolate-brown, tin-plate were more generally known as ferrotypes, or, in America, tintypes. They could be coated, exposed, processed and handed to the customer in little over a minute. After its use in studios in the 1850s and 1860s, the ferrotype process was largely employed by itinerant, fairground booth or beach photographers, especially after the introduction of dry ferrotype plates by L. Nievsky in 1891. This was followed by the development of cameras with built-in processing facilities, removing the need for a portable darktent.

Ferrotypes, although cheap and rapidly produced, were generally of poor quality, although early examples made in proper studios may be quite good. The ferrotype plate is often found loose, and can be easily identified. In a case or a sealed paper mount, it may be identified sometimes by the presence of rust 'blisters' on the image surface, or rust marks on the mount's backing paper. The tinplate's attraction to a magnet may help. The surface of the metal plate is rarely as flat and smooth as that of glass used for conventional collodion positives.

FILM NEGATIVES *1888 to date*
The first material to be used as a transparent substitute for glass was cellulose nitrate – celluloid. A highly inflammable material, it was first used to make sheet films by John Carbutt of Philadelphia in 1888. From the early 1930s, nitrate film was gradually phased out in favour of a safety film, based on non-inflammable cellulose acetate. By the 1950s, the use of nitrate film for photographic materials had ceased. Nitrate film is highly inflammable, especially after its inevitable deterioration reaches a certain critical point. Individual negatives separated from others in well-ventilated storage represent no hazard,

FIG. 4 *Comparison of salted paper and albumen prints, enlarged.* A *Salted paper print, with paper fibres clearly visible.* B *Albumen print, showing a smoother surface and finer detail.* FIG. 5 *Scanning electron micrograph of the surface of albumen paper* × *300. The underlying paper fibres can be seen through cracks in the coating of albumen.* FIG. 6 *Relief image on the carbon print.* A *Carbon print* carte de visite *(Howarth-Loomes Collection).* B *Detail, lit to show the strong relief on details of the image.*
FIG. 7 *Collodion positive image. The negative nature of the image can be seen on the left, against a white background. The black backing on the right shows it as a positive.* FIG. 8 *Relievo process.* A *A collodion positive in which the figure appears to stand out from the background.* B *The effect is produced by using black paint only behind the figure.*

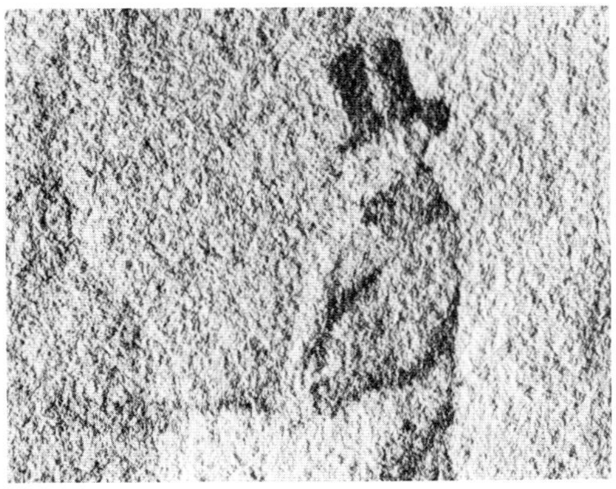

4A

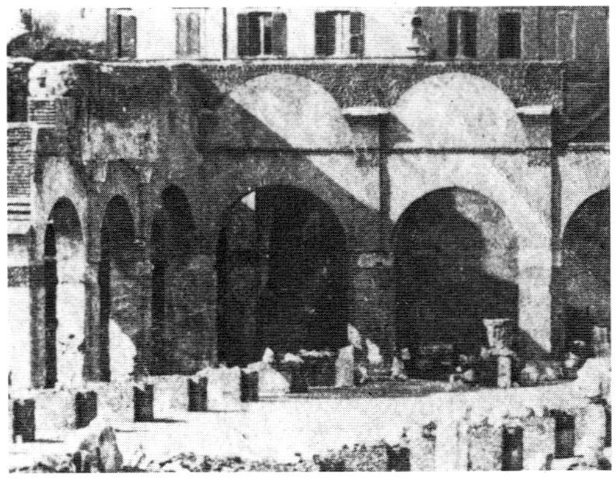

4B

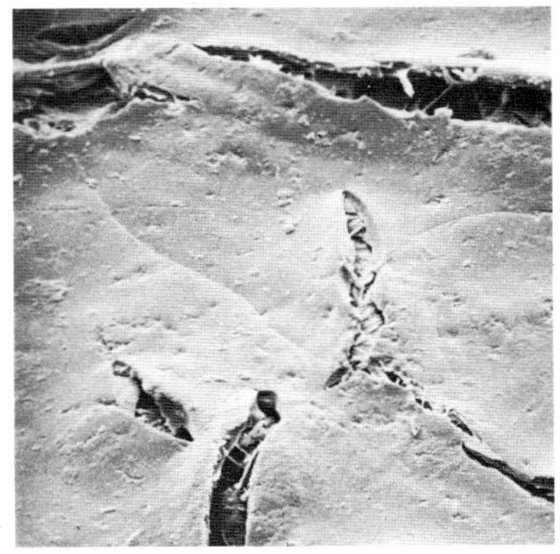

5

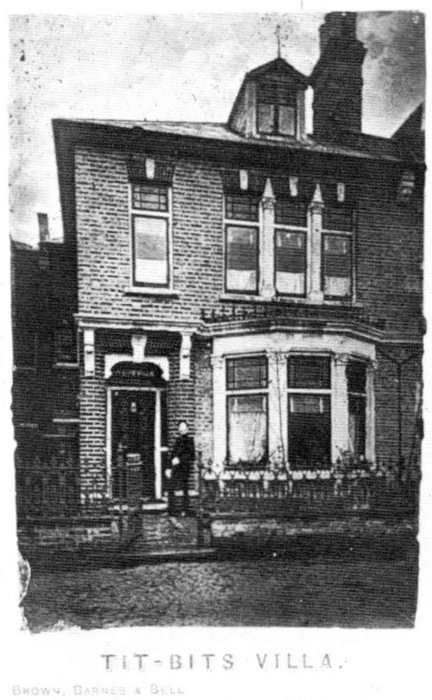

6A

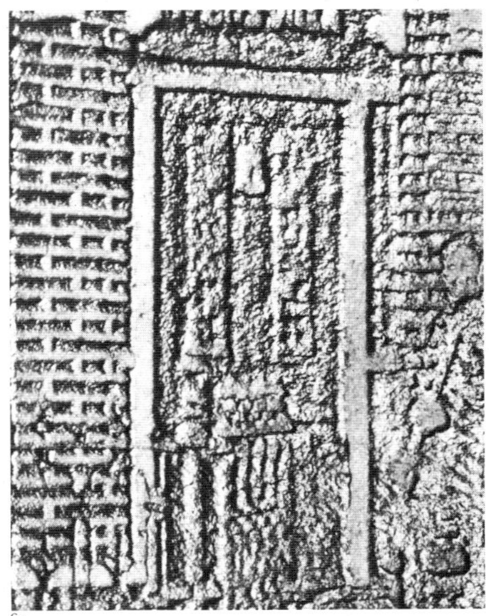

6B

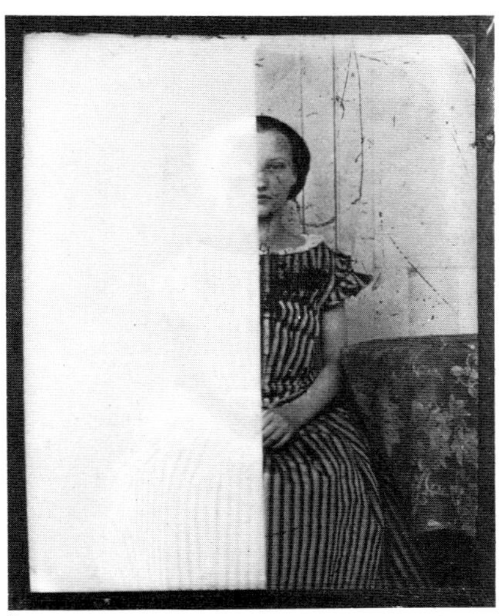

7

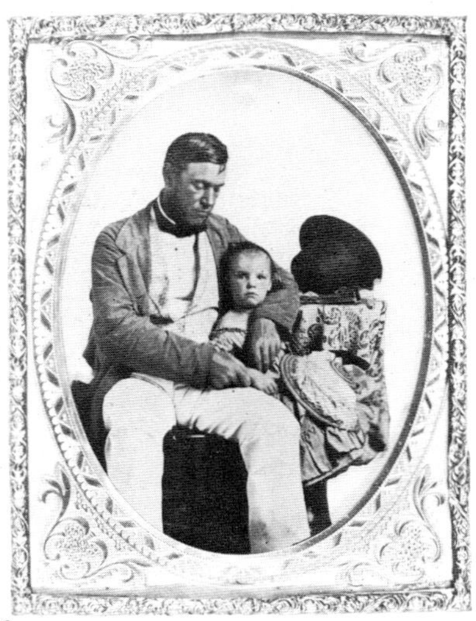

8A

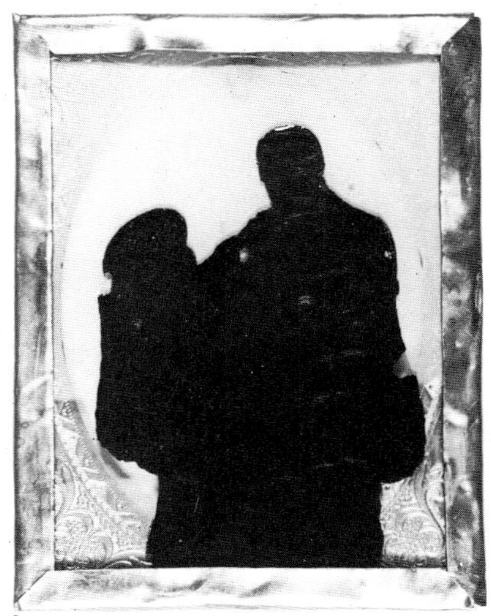

8B

FIG. 9 *The Daguerreotype image.* A *Showing a clear positive image when reflecting a dark ground.* B *Showing as a negative when the ground is light.* FIG. 10 *Scanning electron micrograph of the Daguerreotype image* $\times$ *10,000. The tiny particles of mercury-silver amalgam which form the image are clearly seen against the silver surface of the plate. They are easily removed by rubbing or rough handling.* FIG. 11 *Print from a Frena camera negative, showing the characteristic crenellated edge.* FIG. 12 *Roll film negatives, often show patches of black 'fogging' along opposite edges, where light has entered a loosely rolled film.* FIG. 13 *Prints from Autographic Kodak camera negatives showing photographically reproduced writing under each picture. The Autographic cameras and films were sold between 1914 and the early 1930s.*

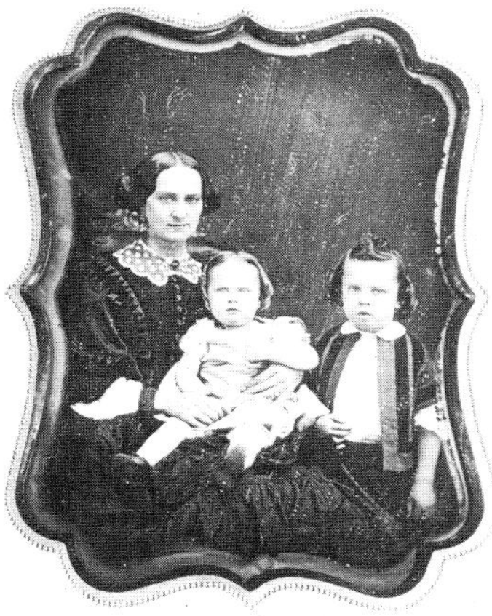

9A

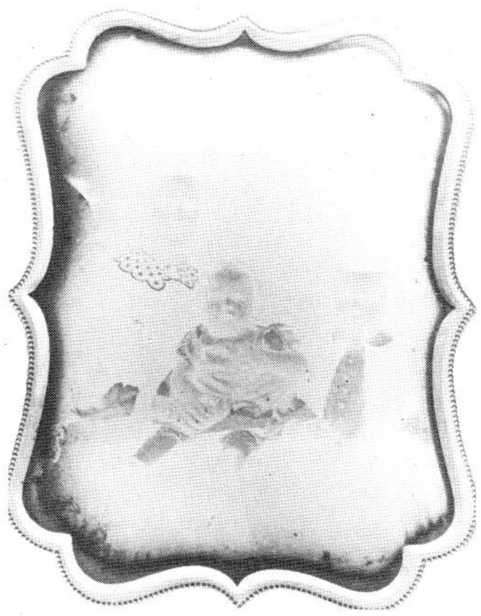

9B

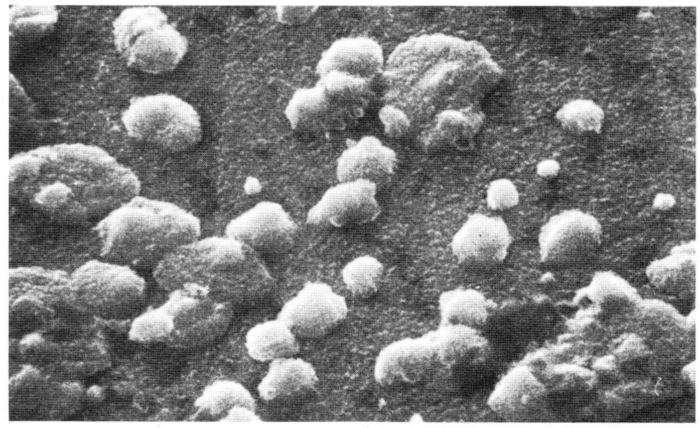

10

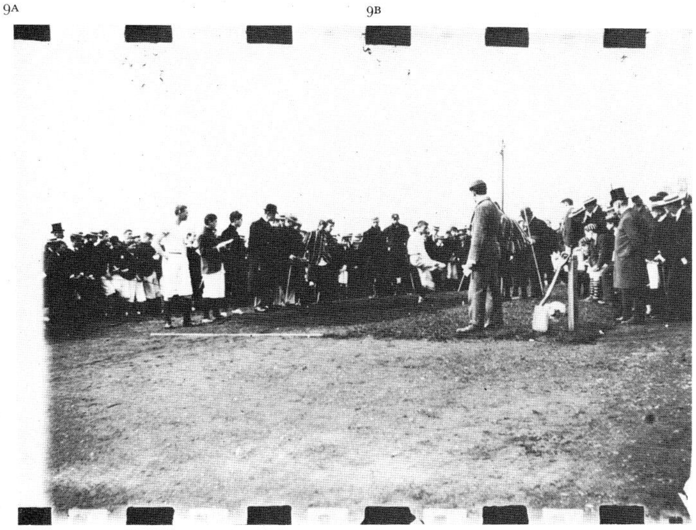

11

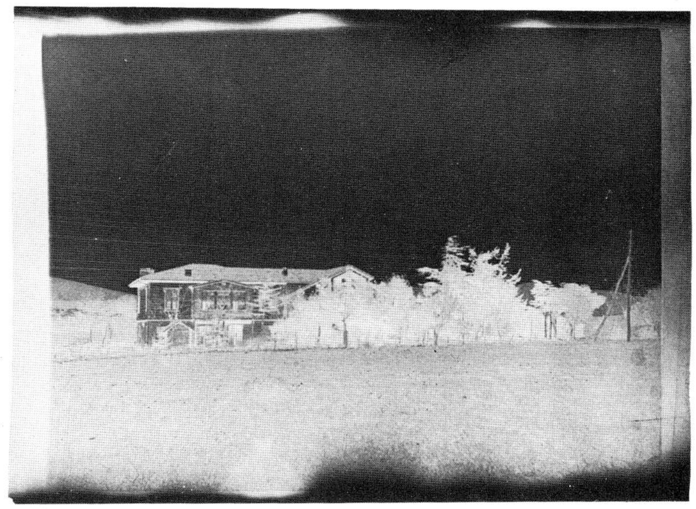

12

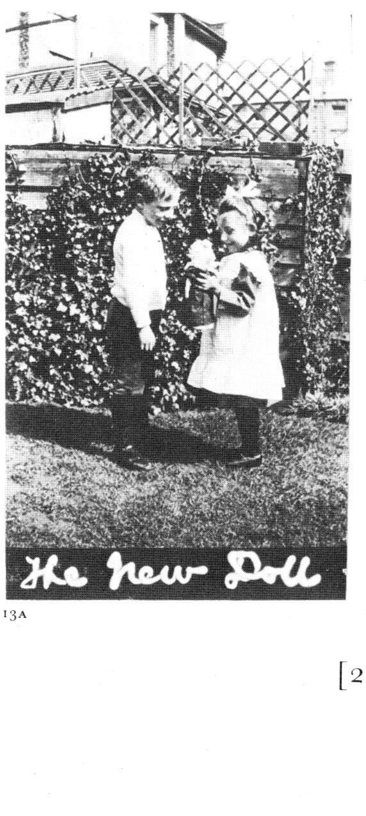

13A

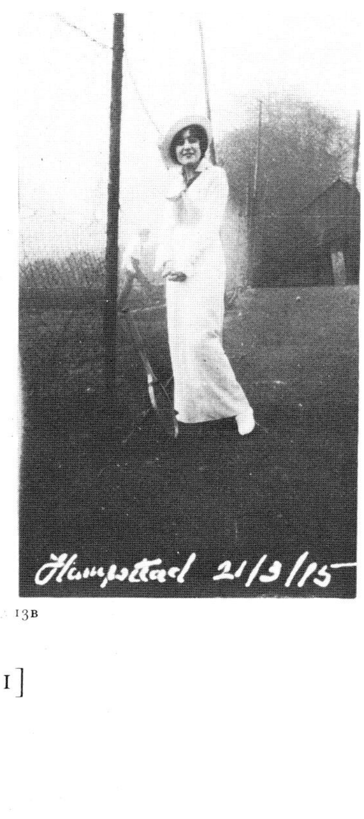

13B

although products of the deterioration might damage nearby negatives. Large quantities of nitrate film tightly packed in sealed containers, in an advanced state of decomposition could self-ignite in prolonged temperatures above 38°C (100°F). Clearly, it is important to identify any large quantities of nitrate in a negative collection. Any film negatives made before 1950 may be suspect. Apart from the burning test given in the key, nitrate film may be identified by dropping a 6mm square of dry film into a test tube containing trichlorethylene, shaking to wet the sample completely. Nitrate film will sink, while acetate and modern polyester films will float.

The first use of film for photographic negatives was the sheet film manufactured by Carbutt in 1888. In this form film saw relatively little use until around the First World War when a gradual change-over began to the use of sheet film instead of glass plates, a change-over not complete until the 1970s. Sheet film on safety base was phased in from 1934, and had almost entirely replaced nitrate film by around 1939. Sheet film negatives are on relatively thick film, so as to be self supporting and flat in the camera. The unusual Frena hand camera, sold from 1892 and popular until the First World War, used packs of sensitised celluloid sheets; the negatives are easily recognised by their castellated ('castle battlements') edges (FIG 11). Uncropped prints may also show signs of this characteristic edge. Sheet film negatives (and uncropped prints made from them), may show manufacturers' names stamped on the edge; 'Nitrate' or 'Safety' may appear on sheet negatives in the 1930s – at least on those of Kodak origin – and coding notches in one edge identify the emulsion side of the film, and from the 1930s, the film type.

The first celluloid roll films were made by George Eastman for his Kodak camera in 1889. The developing popularity of snapshot photography which followed saw a great proliferation in roll film shapes and sizes during the next two decades. Early roll film negatives tend to curl up into a tight roll when dry. In 1904 Eastman introduced non-curl or NC film, in which the tendency of the gelatin emulsion to curl up the film when dry, was counteracted by a plain gelatin coating on the back. The NC film negatives tend to stay flat. Until around 1949 most roll films were on nitrate base; thereafter, safety film was used. Roll film negatives are on thin film. They often show patches of black 'fogging' on opposite edges where light has entered an imperfectly rolled film (FIG 12). Between 1914 and the early 1930s, Autographic Kodak cameras and films permitted the user to 'write' on the film in the camera. The presence of writing in the form of a silver image between successive negatives thus narrows down the likely date. (Uncropped snapshot prints may also show such writing (FIG 13).)

The film pack was invented by J.E. Thornton and was introduced by the Rochester Optical and Camera Company in 1903. A pack of sheet films with a paper tab attached to each enabled each film to be transferred after exposure from the front to the back of the pack by pulling and then tearing off each tab. Film pack negatives can usually be identified by a strip of undeveloped emulsion along one edge, where the paper tab was fastened, and by the much thinner base than that used for ordinary sheet films. Since nitrate film was used for film packs until around 1949, by when they had largely gone out of fashion, any such negatives may be presumed to be on nitrate film.

35mm film for still photography is easily recognised by its width, the usual 24×36mm picture size and the perforations down both edges. Although there were a number of earlier cameras using the film adopted for motion pictures, it was not until after the introduction of the Leica camera in 1925 and the consequent increasing popularity of the miniature camera that there was any significant use of this format. 35mm films for still photographs were on nitrate film up to around 1938.

Some negatives may be on a transparent base other than celluloid. Most often, this will be a sheet of insoluble gelatin. For example, this was used to support negatives stripped from the paper rolls used in the first Kodak cameras, from 1888, and in the earlier roll-holders, from 1886. The Cristoid sheets, sold as glass plate substitutes in the 1890s and 1900s also used insoluble gelatin. Insoluble gelatin 'films' will not burn, and will often be brittle, snapping readily if bent.

FILM PACK *see* FILM NEGATIVES

GELATIN DRY PLATE *1871 to mid 1970s*
The gelatin dry plate process was proposed in 1871 by Dr R.L. Maddox, and after various improvements went into general manufacture from 1878, rapidly replacing the wet collodion process (q.v.). Gelatin dry plates were generally coated by machine, and thus show even coatings right up to the edges of the plate – although deterioration sometimes leads to flaking of the coating at the edges. The image is generally dark by reflected light, although metallic tarnishing of the image may sometimes make it reflective (FIG 15). The negatives are frequently found stored in the manufacturer's boxes. The edges of gelatin plate negatives often show the masking effect of the plate holders in which they were carried in the camera; the earlier collodion negatives normally show an image extending to the very edge of the plate.

GELATIN – SILVER PAPERS *c1880 to date*
The process introduced for the gelatin dry plate (q.v.) was soon applied to papers for printing. The first gelatin based papers were development papers, exposed briefly under a negative and then developed. Papers using silver bromide came into general use around 1880, and have remained in use ever since. Their sensitivity is such as to make practical enlargements by projecting the negative. Slower papers, using silver chloride, appeared about the same time; known as 'Gaslight' papers, they were sensitive enough for contact printing in artificial light, but not for enlarging. The image colour of the chloride print is generally a colder neutral tone than that of a bromide print. Contact papers were generally discontinued in the early 1970s. On both chloride and bromide papers, the developed image was normally black and white, but chemical treatment with one of a variety of toners, usually involving compounds of various metals, could be used to colour the image. Sepia was the most common colour for a toned print, usually on a bromide paper. Development papers could be made in a range of paper thickness, from thin paper to medium card, including postcards, and in base colours including white, ivory and cream as well as on opaque celluloid, usually white. Surface textures could vary from glossy to dead matt, including special surfaces such as silk and even

flock paper (FIG 16). Developed gelatin-silver prints made before the Second World War may show metallic tarnishing on the surface, especially over the darker tones.

Gelatin printing-out papers in use from the mid 1880s often called P.O.P. (a description first used by Ilford Ltd. in 1891), like salted papers (q.v.) and albumen paper (q.v.) were printed in daylight, darkening directly under the action of light. Like all silver printing out processes, P.O.P. prints have a reddish-brown image colour when printed, but frequently they were toned, usually with gold, changing the colour to a purplish-brown, and improving its stability. Untoned prints may have faded partly or wholly to yellow. Most P.O.P. prints had glossy or smooth surfaces, although occasionally matt or textured papers are found. Printing out papers using collodion rather than gelatin as the coating on the paper were in use in the 1890s and 1900s. Most were self-toning papers, containing the necessary salts for toning which took place automatically during the fixing operation. Collodio-chloride papers are not easily distinguished from gelatin printing out papers except by chemical testing, although the collodion layer is less readily affected by moisture and does not become tacky if dampened, as would a gelatin paper. Printing out papers remained in use by amateur and professional photographers at least up to the Second World War, mainly for 'proofing' negatives, although the development papers had largely replaced them for general printing after the 1920s.

GELATIN-SILVER TRANSPARENCY *c1880 to c1970*
A gelatin-silver chloride or bromide emulsion coated on glass, used generally for the making of lantern slides (FIG 14). The image may be black and white or toned; some tarnishing of the silver may be apparent. Discounting this, the image normally is dark by reflection against a dark surface, unlike the albumen or collodion transparencies (q.v.)

GUM BICHROMATE PRINTS *1894 to 1920s*
The gum, or 'bi-gum', process was introduced in 1894 by A. Rouillé-Ladévéze. It used the principle of the selective hardening of paper coated with gum arabic treated with potassium bichromate when exposed to daylight under a negative. The exposed gum layer, containing a pigment, was washed with water, so that the parts rendered insoluble were left behind. The result could be modified greatly by the degree of washing, with local treatment with brushes or water jets, for example, and the print could be re-sensitised and reprinted several times if desired. A wide variety of paper surfaces could be employed; rough surfaces were popular. Gum prints show little resolution of fine detail, and rather broad tonal effects. They may resemble crayon or charcoal drawings. Almost any pigment colour could be employed.

The process was very popular with pictorial photographers in the 1890s and 1900s for exhibition print making. It had gone out of general use by the 1930s, although today it is undergoing something of a revival.

HALF-TONE PRINTING *1880s to date*
The principle of the breaking up of a photographic image into small dots to facilitate making a printing plate was suggested by W.H.F. Talbot in 1852, but it did not receive commercial application until the early 1880s. In various forms it has remained in use to the present day for the production of long printing runs of reproduced photographs. Half-tone reproductions are easily recognised by the regular dot or line structure visible, if not with the naked eye, with the aid of a lens.

INSOLUBLE GELATIN FILM *see* FILM NEGATIVES

METOTYPE PRINTS *1890s to 1900s*
Gelatin-silver emulsions coated on papers coated with metal powders were used for making decorative prints. Gold, silver, copper and bronze finishes are found, and some may be additionally tinted with colours. Also known as Metalotypes. In recent years similar papers have been marketed.

NITRATE FILM *see* FILM NEGATIVES

NON-CURL FILM *see* FILM NEGATIVES

OIL PIGMENT PRINT *1904 to 1910s*
A process, described by G.E.H. Rawlins in 1904, using a gelatin coated paper treated with potassium bichromate and exposed to daylight under a negative. The selective hardening of the gelatin which occurred affected its ability to absorb fatty inks or oil-based pigments which were dabbed on with a brush – a procedure which gave some measure of control over the final result. The print could be dried and left, or the ink transferred while wet to another sheet under pressure. The process was suitable only for contact printing; enlargements could be made by the Bromoil process (q.v.). Like all the similar pigment processes, the oil pigment print generally shows limited resolution and broad tonal effects.

OPALINES *1890s to 1900s*
A gelatin-silver print, usually P.O.P., was stuck face down on a thick sheet of bevelled-edged glass, often with gilt edge, and backed with white or coloured paper. The whole might be set in a plush mount. It was a popular method of preparing decorative photographs at the turn of the century.

OPALOTYPES *1880s to 1900s*
Photograph on opal (white) glass. The print could be produced by carbon printing (q.v.) or by printing or enlarging a negative on opal glass sensitised with a gelatin-bromide emulsion. The two may be distinguished by the presence of fading or tarnishing on the black and white silver image, and the generally warmer tones of the carbon print, which may show traces of the relief image, and the edges of the transferred film may be visible within the edges of the opal plate. Opalotypes, or Opal prints, were frequently coloured and framed, and were especially popular in the 1890s and 1900s.

PAPER NEGATIVES
Apart from the early use of paper in the Calotype and Waxed Paper processes (q.v.), some use of paper for negative making was made in later years. George Eastman introduced a rapid gelatin-silver negative paper in 1883 as a light-weight substitute for glass plates. The paper sheets were placed in a special adaptor to fit in the camera plate-holder, and the 'shadow' of the U-shaped adaptor may be visible on three of the four edges

FIG. 14 *Transparencies.* A *Gelatin-silver lantern slide, dark by reflected light.*
B *Albumen or collodion lantern slide, giving a light, negative image by reflected light.*
FIG. 15 *Comparison of wet collodion and gelatin dryplate negatives.*
A *By reflected light – the collodion negative (right) appears light, and positive in character; the gelatin negative looks dark.* B *By transmitted light, the gelatin plate shows even coating and the 'shadow' of the plate holder at the edge; the uneven coating of the collodion negative and the cracking and flaking of the coating (this is an extreme example) are seen on the right.*

14A

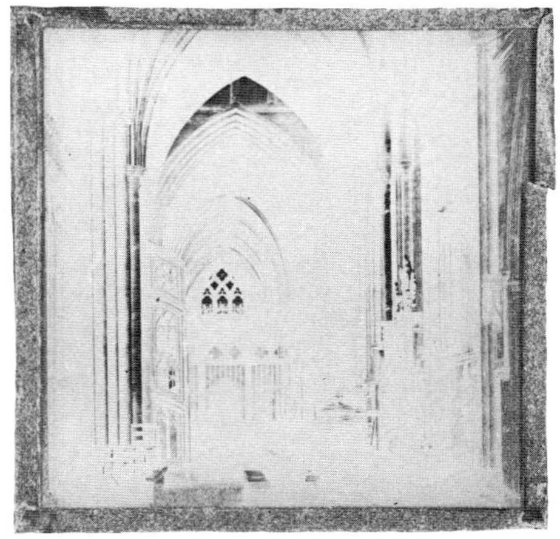

14B

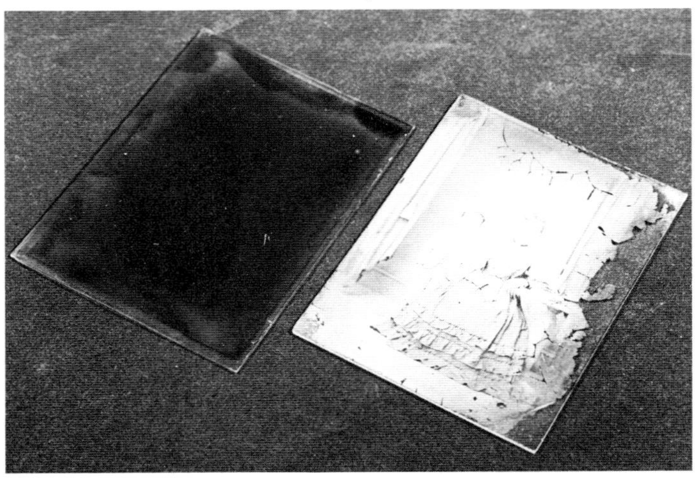

15A

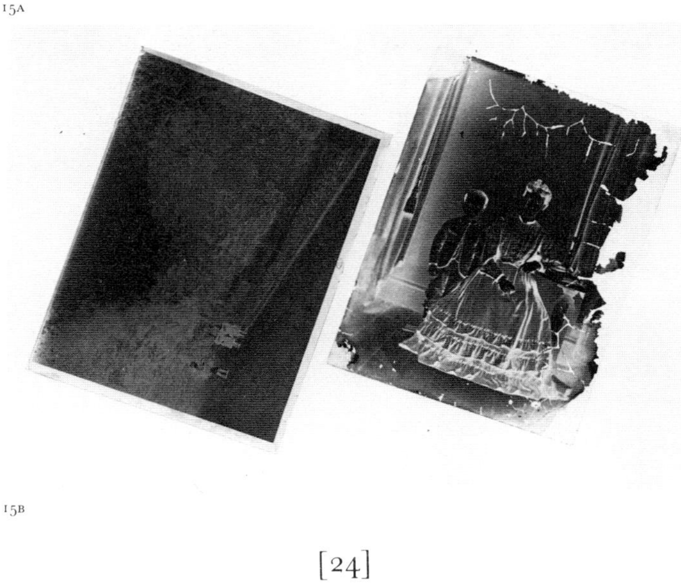

15B

FIG. 16 *Comparison of bromide paper surfaces, enlarged (notice progressive loss of detail).* A *Glossy – with a strong light reflection on the left, and showing fine detail.* B *Matt – with no surface reflection, but some loss of detail.* C *Rough – with a textured surface, but significant loss of detail.* D *Crayon – with a stronger texturing of the surface.*

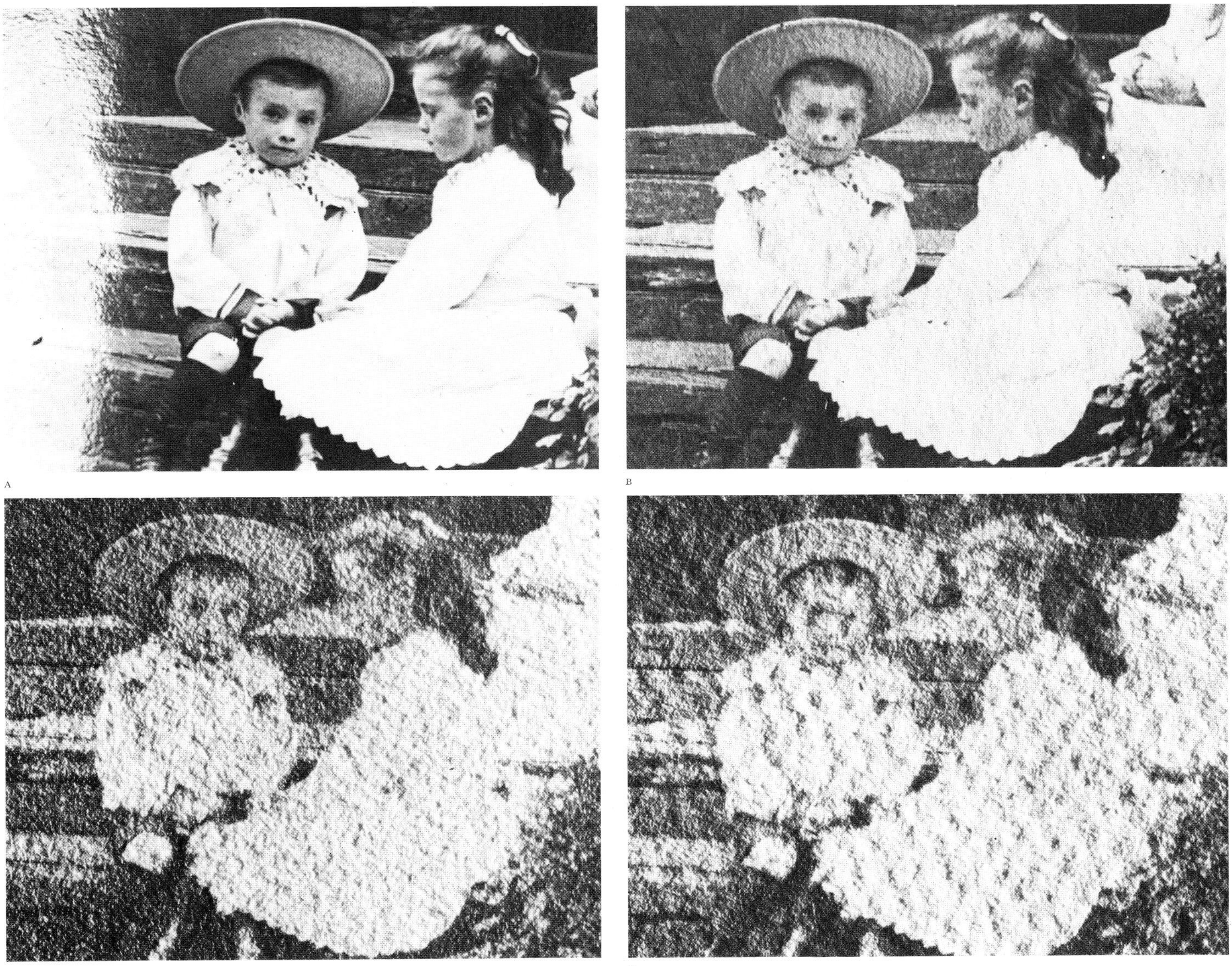

A B C D

FIG. 17 *Comparison of prints from paper and glass negatives.* A *Bramhall Hall – developed salted paper print from a waxed paper negative and detail.* B *James Nasmyth and his steam hammer – developed salted paper print from a wet collodion negative and detail.* C. *Bramhall Hall – albumen print from a wet collodion negative and detail.*

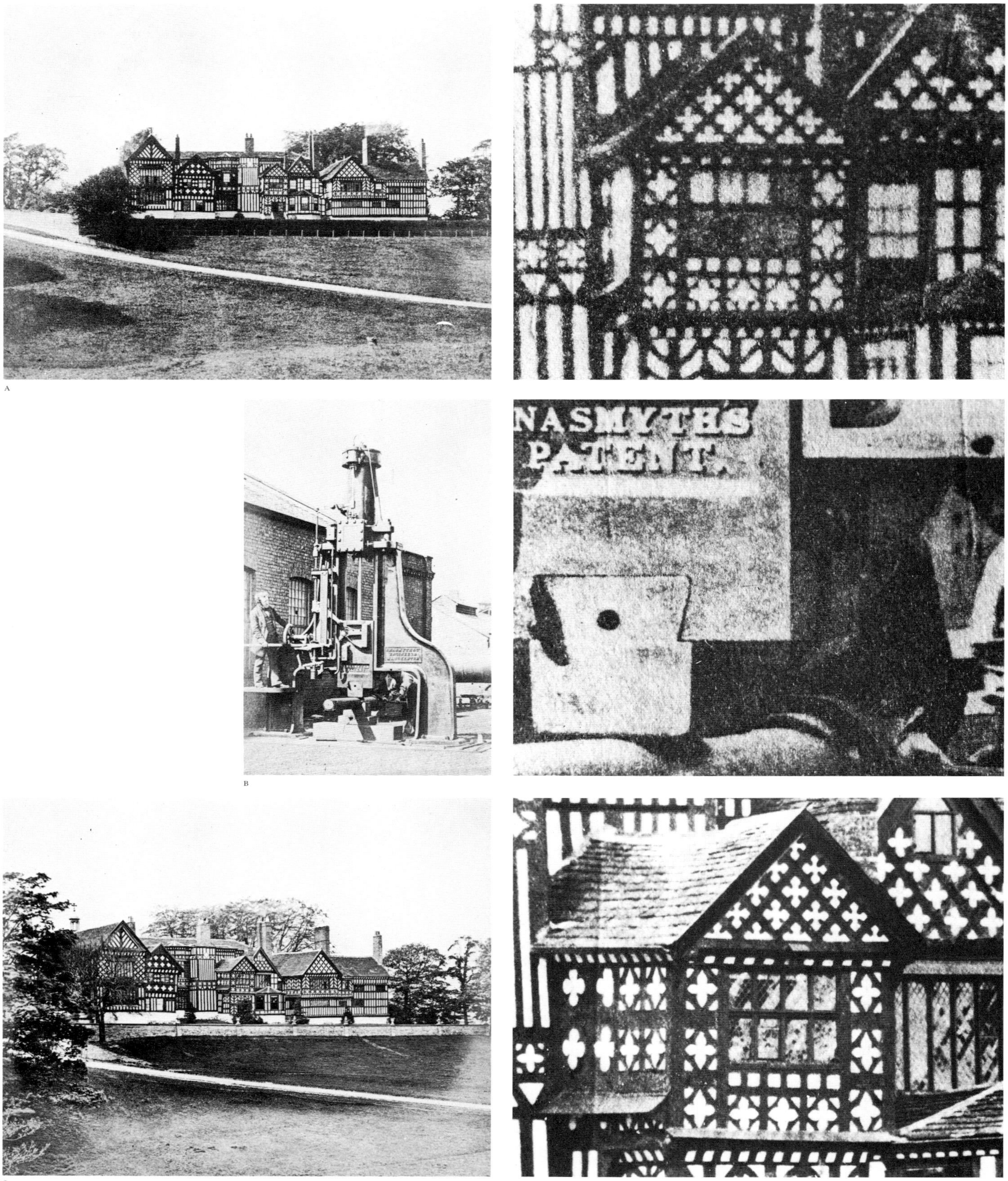

of the negative. In 1884 the paper was available in rolls for a roll-holder adaptor sold by Eastman, but it was soon replaced by an alternative paper in which the emulsion could be stripped from the paper after processing, and transferred to a transparent support. Negatives made on the Eastman Negative paper may be translucent and of a yellow colour, since it was usual to oil them before printing.

Pictorial photographers in the 1890s and 1900s sometimes used paper negatives (frequently copy negatives) for the softening of detail and effect of paper texture. Generally such negatives are of larger size. Small, snapshot size negatives may date from the 1900s when cheap paper roll films were on the market. Even as late as the 1940s and 1950s paper based rollfilms were supplied by 'free film' processing houses.

In the 1920s and 1930s thin sensitised negative cards were available for use in the camera, printed by reflection printing in special enlargers.

PHOTOCERAMICS
A burnt-in impression of a photograph in the glaze on china, porcelain, earthenware or enamelled metal could be by one of several methods, the earliest of which dates from the mid 1850s. Carbon transfer printing, using enamel colours as pigments, was one method. Protected by the glaze, such pictures are completely protected from abrasion or the effects of even hot water, and may be found on dinnerplates, cups and glasses. Carbon transfer printing (q.v.) could be used to apply an image to the surface only of a ceramic material, but the image would be much more vulnerable.

PHOTOGRAVURE PRINTS *c1880 to date*
A development of a photomechanical printing process invented by W.H.F. Talbot in 1858, which came into use in a commercial form around 1880, after improvements by Karel Klic. In its original form, photogravure used a copper plate dusted with fine ashphaltum powder then coated with a bichromated gelatin 'tissue' of the type used in carbon printing (q.v.). The exposed and selectively hardened layer controlled the penetration of an etching solution, so that the printing plate was etched to different depths. Inked, it was used to transfer the image to a suitable paper. The lack of any regular or well defined image structure distinguishes it from other photomechanical printing methods. Photogravure was used for quality reproduction of the work of many of the best-known pictorial photographers in the 1890s and 1900s.

PLATINUM PRINTS OR PLATINOTYPES *1873 to c1920*
Invented by William Willis in 1873, materials for the process were marketed from 1879. Plain paper containing light sensitive iron salts, (but no silver), and a platinum compound was exposed in contact with a negative to daylight. The exposed print was developed in a solution of potassium oxalate, finely divided platinum metal being deposited in the paper to form the image. The finely divided platinum was intensely black, and the platinum print shows characteristic rich blacks and completely neutral, almost silvery-grey mid tones. By developing the print in a hot developer a warmer, almost sepia platinum image was produced. Platinum printing went out of fashion after the First World War due to a dramatic rise in the cost of the metal. In recent years the process has been revived by some photographers.

Platinum prints are generally recognisable by their image colour and plain paper surface. In the 1890s and 1900s manufacturers of gelatin-silver papers tried to match the characteristics of the platinum print with their products. 'Platino-matt' prints, if in good condition, can resemble the real thing, but usually some image deterioration will be present. If a very small sample from the edge of a print is available, it can be tested by applying a drop of a solution made from 25gms of mercuric chloride and 5ml hydrochloric acid in 1 litre of water. Silver prints will bleach, platinum prints will not. Platinum prints in albums may sometimes be identified by a rust-coloured impression of the picture on a facing page, formed by residual iron salts diffusing from the platinum paper.

PRINTING OUT PAPERS *see* GELATIN-SILVER PAPERS

REFLECTION PRINTING NEGATIVES *see* PAPER NEGATIVES

SAFETY FILM *see* FILM NEGATIVES

SALTED PAPER PRINTS *1839 to c1855; 1890s to 1900s*
W.H.F. Talbot in 1834 discovered that plain writing paper treated with a common salt solution and sensitised with silver nitrate became light-sensitive, darkening when exposed to light. He used his 'photogenic drawing' paper to make prints of leaves and lace, and in 1835 took camera pictures of his home at Lacock. He published details of his process in 1839. The plain salted paper was used to make prints in his improved Calotype process (q.v.). Salted paper was superseded in the 1850s by albumen paper (q.v.), but enjoyed a revival in the 1890s and 1900s, when it was popular with pictorial photographers, since any rough or textured paper could be sensitised. Like all printing-out processes, salted paper gave images of a reddish-brown colour. Although the prints are quite stable to light, the unprotected silver image is very vulnerable to airborne pollutants, and the prints are frequently faded to yellow at the edges, or all over. The uncoated paper surface is characteristic; very lightly albumenised prints may be confused with salted paper prints, especially if faded, but the albumen print will generally show distinctly yellow highlights.

SHEET FILM *see* FILM Negatives

TRANSFEROTYPE PRINT *1888 to 1940s*
A gelatin-silver emulsion coated on paper from which it could be stripped after its exposure and processing and transferred to another paper, or any other surface. The normal black and white image could be toned to other colours. The silver image may show signs of tarnishing or deterioration, unlike carbon prints (q.v.).

WAXED PAPER NEGATIVES *1851 to c1865*
A variant of the calotype process (q.v.), published in 1851 by Gustave le Gray. The paper was waxed before sensitising, improving its transparency, but more importantly, improving its keeping properties so that it could be prepared many days before use and in addition increased its capacity to record finer detail (FIG 17). It was rather slower than the calotype process, exposures of 15 minutes or more being not uncommon for landscapes, and development times running into hours were

usual. The process was especially popular in Britain and France, although, like the calotype, it was hardly used in America. It rivalled the contemporary wet collodion process (q.v.) for some years, having the advantage of not requiring a portable darktent on location. It is extremely difficult to establish whether a waxed negative has been so prepared before or after sensitising; but it is reasonable to assume that if made before 1851 the negative will be a calotype, while waxed negatives made in later years were probably made by the waxed paper process.

Woodburytypes *1865 to c1900*
W.B. Woodbury patented this process in 1865. A relief image was made in bichromated gelatin, as in the carbon process (q.v.), and was placed in an hydraulic press in contact with a block of lead, in which was produced a mould in shallow relief, following the contours of the picture. The block was coated with gelatinous ink which was transferred to paper in a press. The Woodburytype print shows no grain or image structure, and has all the subtlety of tone of a true photograph. Woodburytypes were used extensively for book illustrations in the 1870s and 1880s; they will be found mounted on book pages or printed card mounts, almost invariably bearing a process credit 'Woodburytype' or, in France 'Photoglyptie'. The image often shows a visible relief, especially true in the case of Woodburytype transparencies on glass made as lantern slides. Woodburytypes are normally of a chocolate brown colour, but any other pigment colour could be used.

Span of Formats and Processes

● *period of greatest use* ○ *period of lesser use* · *period of limited use*

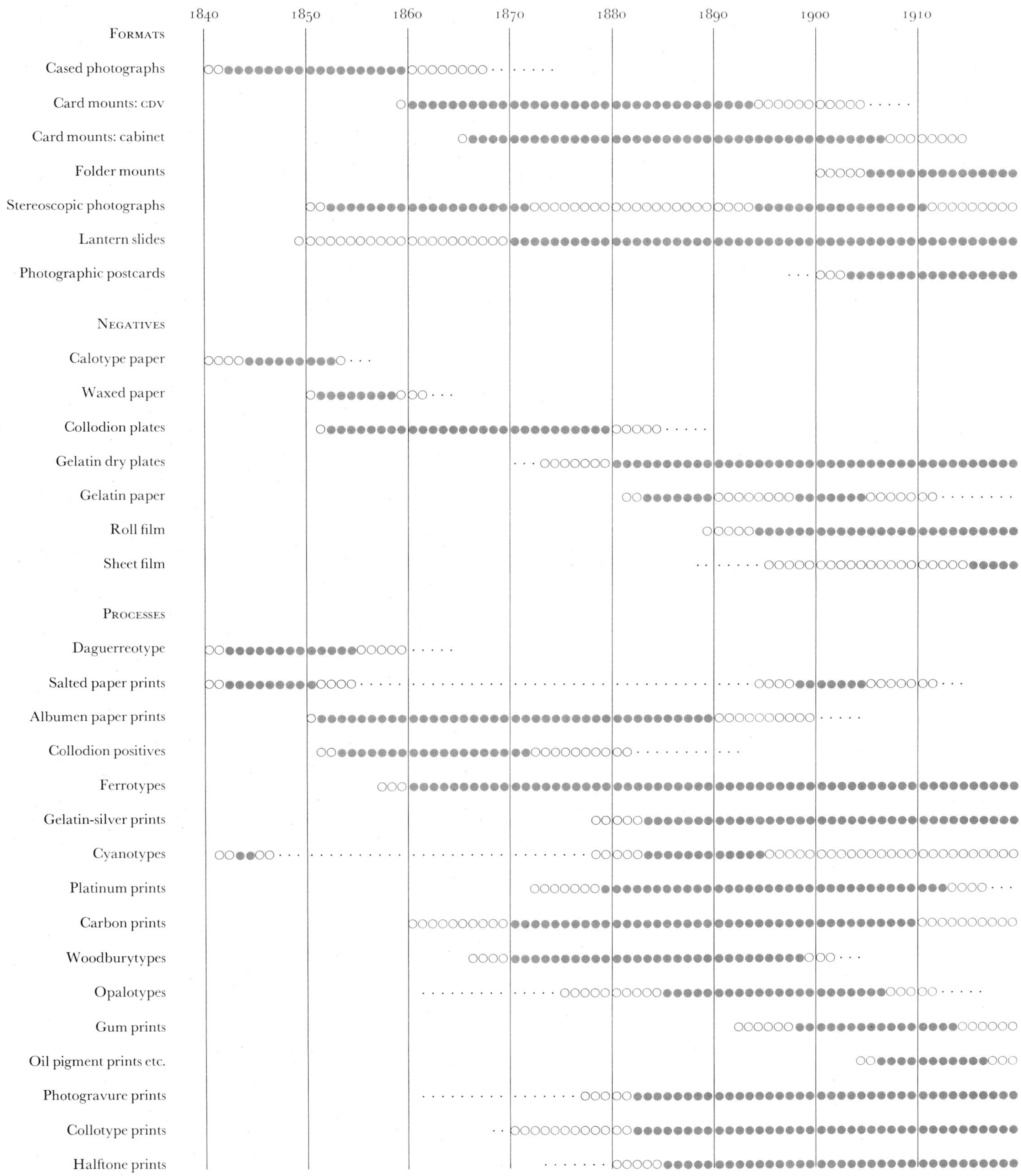

THE PLATES AND COMMENTARY

*The plates are arranged in terms of their chemical and physical classes rather than chronologically. Silver prints are placed first (*PLATES *1–22), followed by iron-based processes (*PLATES *23–25), and then processes using pigments including printing inks (*PLATES *26–37).*

PLATE

1

Anonymous photographer
Portrait of Egerton Cleeve Late 1840s
Hand-tinted Daguerreotype in papier-maché case, plush-lined
120 × 88mm Mus. no. 7–1973

The Daguerreotype process was introduced in 1839, and after various improvements came into widespread use from 1841, principally for portraiture. The image, in the form of a greyish deposit on a polished silver surface, can be seen as a positive only if the plate is held so as to reflect a dark ground. When the Daguerreotype was over-exposed in the camera, as could happen with areas of very white clothing, or in sky areas in exteriors, solarisation could occur, in which the lightest areas became darker. This accounts for the bluish colour of the shirt front of the sitter in this photograph. The physical nature of the Daguerreotype image made it prone to damage if touched, and the processed plate was usually sealed in a mount with a matt (or mask) and a cover glass. The whole was set in a hanging frame or, more often, in a leather or moulded paper covered case. This example is unusual in that the plate has been cut to an oval to match the mount. Each Daguerreotype was unique; if more than one copy was needed, extra photographs were taken, or the original had to be copied by re-photographing.

The Daguerreotype image is normally laterally reversed, giving a mirror image of the sitter. Rarely, this was corrected by taking the picture through a prism or via a mirror. The silver surface is likely to have become tarnished if the sealing has been imperfect, and this may be seen as an iridescent tarnishing usually at the edges of the picture. It can be seen on this example.

While leading Daguerreotype studios often identified their production by embossing the case with the studio's name and address, or inserting a printed slip beneath the plate, or inscribing the image surface with a signature, most Daguerreotypes are, like this one, anonymous. Sometimes the name of the sitter was engraved on the cover glass, scratched on the back of the plate or written on a piece of paper pasted to the cover. However, most subjects of Daguerreotypes are now as anonymous as their makers. This example carried an inscription: 'Daguerreotype of the late Egerton Cleeve, 5th and youngest son of late Lt. Col. W. Cleeve RA. Born 9 August 1827. Died 1850 at Monte Video of yellow fever unmarried'. The main function of the process was to record loved ones.

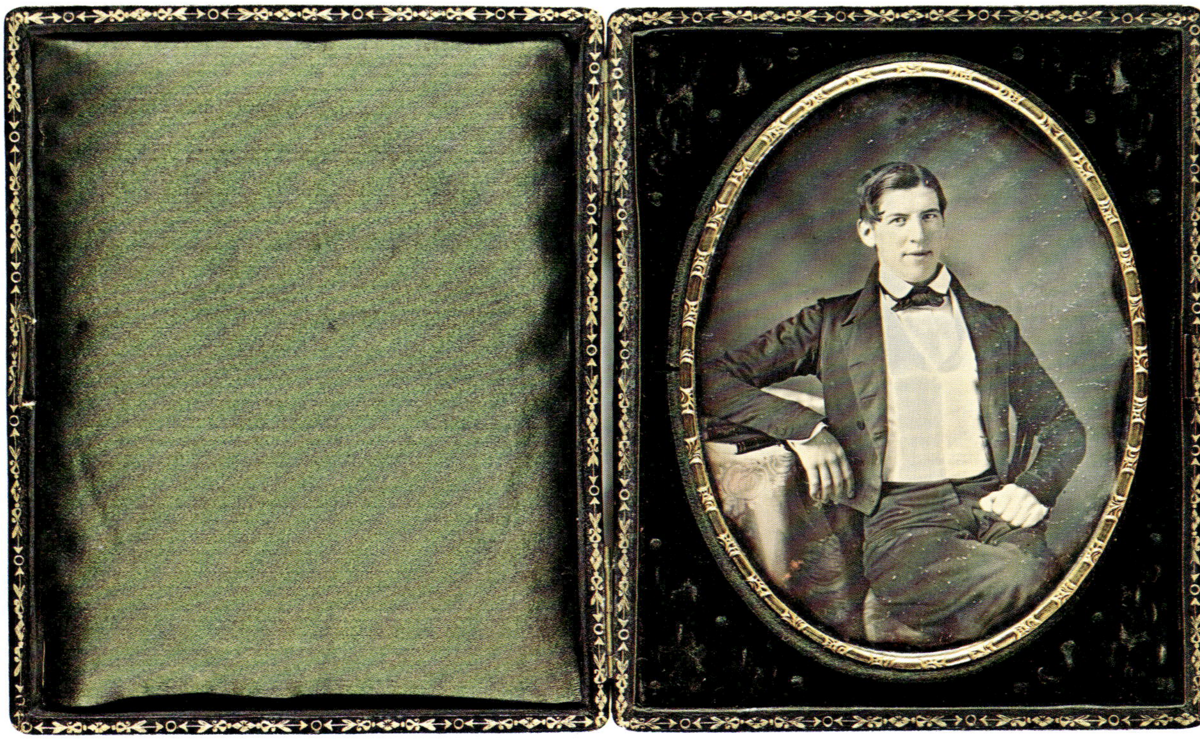

PLATE

2

William Edward Kilburn British Active 1846–62
Portrait of Martha Emma Roper (1818–65) About 1851
Hand-tinted and gilt Daguerreotype in plush-lined papier-maché case, embossed with the studio's name and the Royal arms
Image size 90 × 65 mm (reproduced same size) Mus. no. 1–1939 Given by J.L. Nevinson

The neutral grey tones of the Daguerreotype put it at a disadvantage with the miniature painting. *Blackwood's Magazine* in 1842 commented 'The likenesses produced . . . are so absolutely fearful, that we have but little hope of ever seeing anything tolerable from any machine. It must want colour . . . and its best likeness can be only that of a rigid bust, or a corpse'. For this reason, it was a common practice to add colour by hand. Often this would be no more than a touch of gilding on jewellery, or a faint flesh tint on hands or face. Sometimes, much more elaborate colouring was employed; colouring Daguerreotypes was a skilled business, since the fragile image could not be brushed over with heavy paint. In the main, one of two methods would be used. One involved the careful dusting-on of dry powder colour mixed with dry gum, which was fixed on the plate by breathing on it, a method patented by Richard Beard in 1842. Alternatively, colours mixed in alcohol could be painted on with care, drying rapidly to a transparent tint, a method introduced by Antoine Claudet. Colouring outfits cost from half a guinea for ten colours, including gold and silver, to two guineas for a box of 36 colours with all necessary implements.

For the first five years of commercial Daguerreotyping in London the medium was controlled as a near monopoly by Richard Beard. In 1846 he issued licenses to, among others, W.E. Kilburn, whose studio at 234 Regent Street offered the painted portrait Daguerreotype as a speciality: 'the likeness taken by the photographic process serves merely as a sketch for the miniature, which is painted by M. Mansion . . . . They have, when finished, all the delicacy of an elaborate miniature with the infallible accuracy of expression obtained by the photographic process' (from an advertisement in *The Athenaeum* 10 April 1847). There was stiff competition among the leading studios for the best miniature painters; the combination of high quality Daguerreotypes and overpainting flourished until the closure of the studios of Kilburn and his great rival Claudet in 1862. Both studios were awarded medals at the Great Exhibition of 1851. That is the traditional date given to this portrait, which is supported by the style of the sitter's dress.

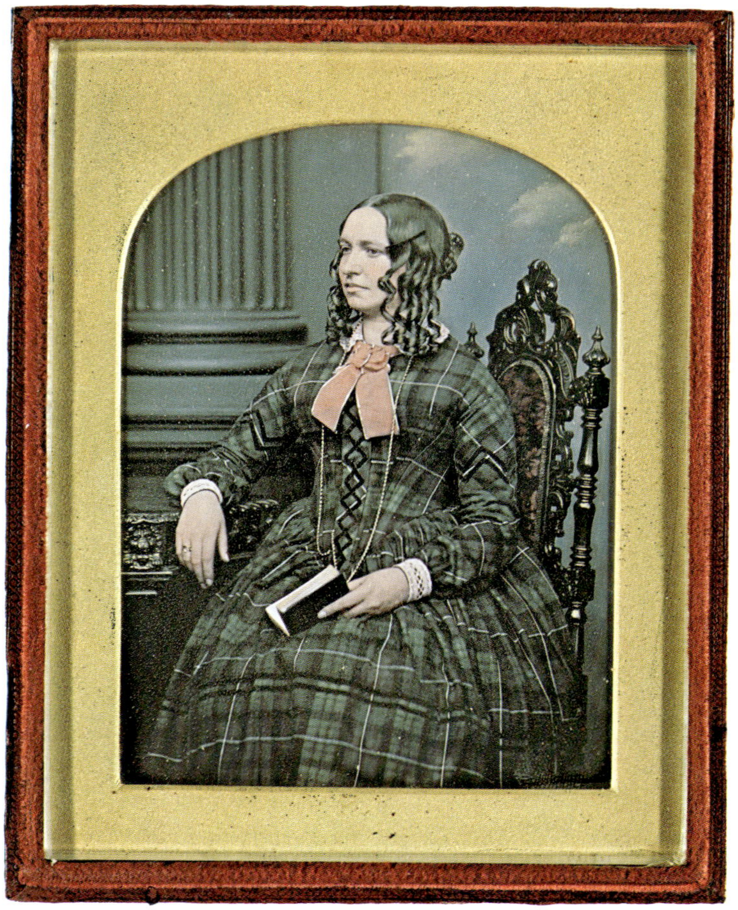

PLATE

3

Anonymous American photographer
Gustav Adolf Hiller, his wife Julia and their daughter Luise 1851–52
Daguerreotype in papier-maché case painted and inlaid with mother of pearl
Image size 122 × 88 *mm (reproduced same size)* *Mus. no.* 263–1975 *Purchase*

The Daguerreotype process required skilful manipulation in the sensitising and developing operations, but the key to success lay in the polishing of the plate. The better the polish, the finer was the quality. Hand polishing using leather buffs and jeweller's rouge was the method generally employed in England, and considerable effort and care were needed to get a first class finish. As might be expected, many American photographers mechanised the process, polishing their plates on steam-power-driven buffing machines. The mirror-like surface required could be produced in a short time and this is the main reason for the high average quality of American Daguerreotypes. American Daguerreotypists took three out of the five prizes awarded for the process in the photographic section which was part of the Great Exhibition of 1851. Daguerreotypes polished with rotary buffs do not normally show the fine parallel lines produced by hand polishing in which the plate was slid backwards and forwards on the polishing buff.

This family portrait is labelled on the back in German by one of the children of the child in the picture. The label also dates the Daguerreotype and mentions where it was taken – Cincinnati. The case is painted with flowers, decorated with tortoiseshell, and got up as a book – with the word Friendship on the 'spine'.

A historian of Cincinnati, Charles Cist, wrote in 1851 that the city had 37 Daguerreotypists plus 78 assistants. He noted with pride: 'Our Daguerrian artists stand high everywhere . . . their works were recognized at a glance in Florence, by Frenchmen and others, as American productions, and superior to anything produced on the continent of Europe'. One Cincinnati establishment was described at length in 1854. Its opulent setting was surmounted by a painted ceiling with 'a centre piece representing the aerial regions, in which Venus, the goddess of Beauty, is sitting recumbent on a splendid throne . . . . The very seat on which you sit and the carpet on which you tread seem to be a gem culled from the fragrant lap of Flora' (*Gleason's Pictorial Drawing-Room Companion* 1 April 1854). Such were the surroundings in which families – proudly, nervously or unselfconsciously – returned the camera's stare. The resulting picture might cause misgivings on the part of one or more of the sitters but the silvered plate itself was usually regarded with wonderment:

> 'Here's a present I got for you in New York.' It was a Daguerreotype, clear and soft as an engraving, representing Eva and her father sitting hand in hand. (Harriet Beecher Stowe, *Uncle Tom's Cabin* 1852).

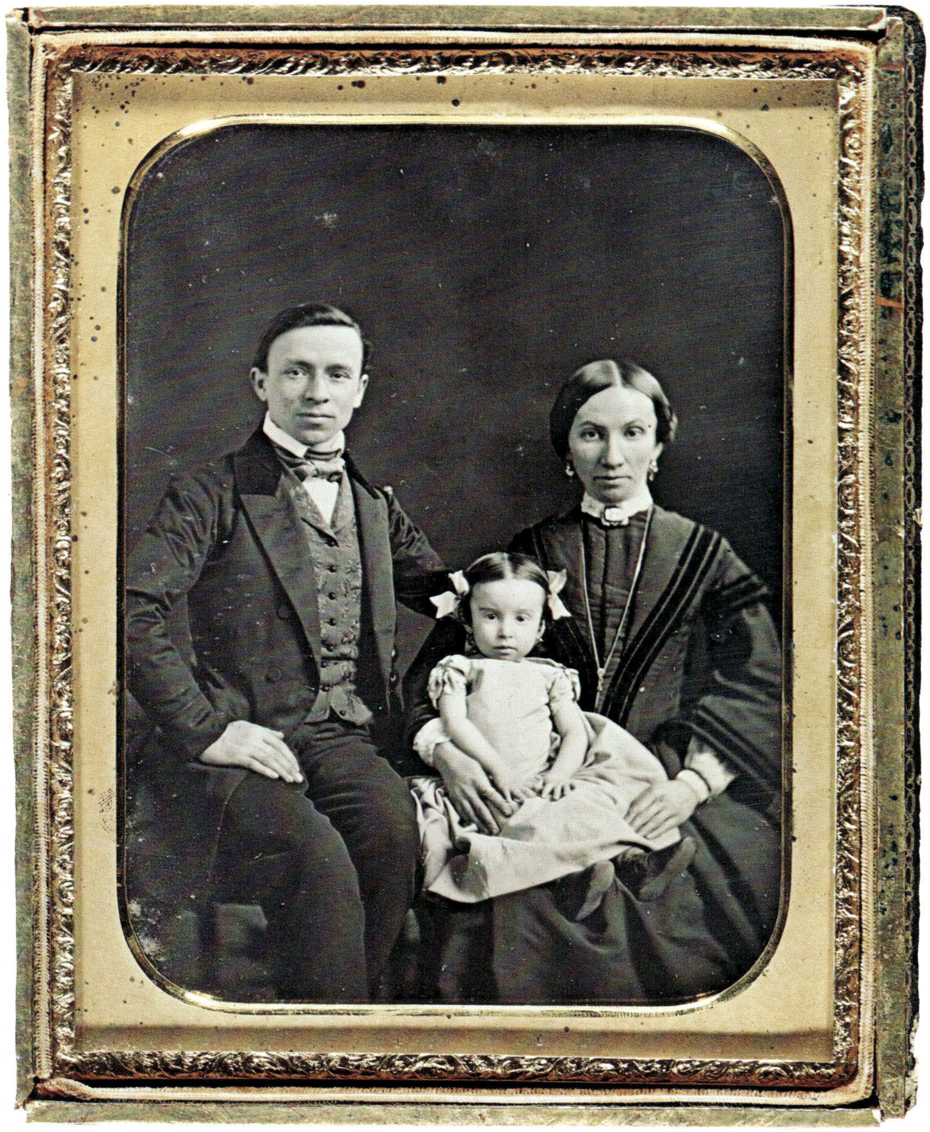

PLATE

4

Anonymous photographer
Father and child 1850s
Hand-tinted collodion positive (Relievo variant)
Image size 87 × 65 mm (reproduced same size) The Kodak Museum

Anonymous photographer
Mary Sophia Nevinson (1847–1937) Late 1850s
Hand-tinted collodion positive in papier-maché plush-lined case
Image size 68 × 54 mm (reproduced same size) Mus. no. Ph. 310–1982
Given by J.L. Nevinson

The collodion positive was a less expensive form of photograph than the Daguerreotype, although it was also a unique image, and usually also laterally reversed. The whitish negative image was backed with black to give the effect of a positive. Usually this was done with black paint applied to the back of the glass plate, as in this example. The plate was usually covered with a brass matt and cover glass, held together by a brass foil frame. The mounted plate was supplied in a hanging frame or case similar to those used for Daguerreotypes, although often of inferior quality. The collodion image usually remains in good condition if protected, although sometimes the edges may be tarnished. On the other hand, the black backing paint may crack or flake off, giving the impression that the image is damaged (as in the baby's head illustrated). The Relievo variant of the process is described in the Glossary.

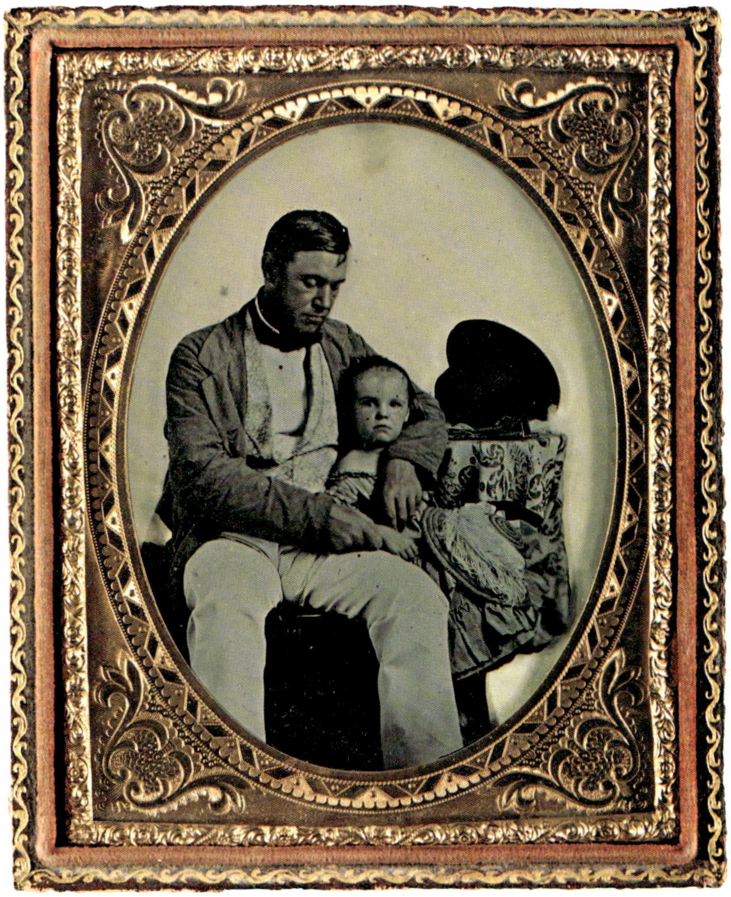

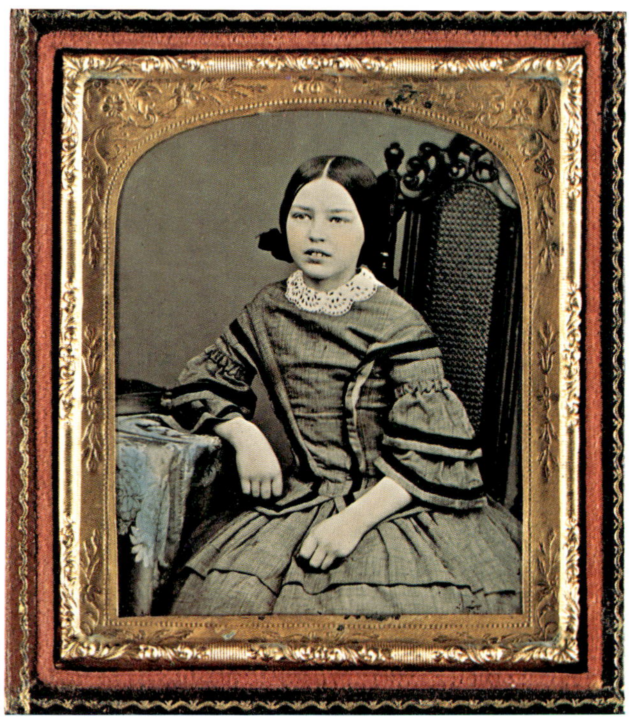

PLATE

5

William Henry Fox Talbot British 1800–77
The Open Door April 1844
Calotype positive and negative
140 × 193mm The Science Museum, London

The negative-positive calotype process discovered by W.H.F. Talbot in 1840 and published and patented by him in 1841 was the beginning of photography in the form we know it. Talbot had made camera negatives and printed from them as early as 1835, but his improved process, with its manageably short exposure times, made it a rival to the Daguerreotype process. In practice, the paper negative, relatively inexpensive, even in large sizes, and requiring only simple preparation was especially attractive to amateur photographers, particularly for landscape and architectural work, while the Daguerreotype process remained the principal medium for professional portraiture. The advantage of the negative's ability to produce as many copies as required was promoted by Talbot in his six-part publication *The Pencil of Nature*, produced between 1844 and 1846 and illustrated with calotype prints made at Talbot's establishment at Reading. 'The Open Door', PLATE 6, was printed from a paper negative which in this case was unwaxed, although Talbot and his contemporaries often waxed the negative after processing to make it translucent, cutting down the printing time. The print, on salted paper, shows the characteristic reddish-brown colour of the calotype print. Unlike this example, many salted paper prints have faded, often to a yellowish colour, especially at the edges.

The Open Door was published in the second instalment of *The Pencil of Nature* together with Talbot's own commentary:

> The chief object of the present work is to place on record some of the early beginnings of a new art, before the period, which we trust is approaching, of its being brought to maturity by the aid of British talent. This is one of the trifling efforts of its infancy, which some partial friends have been kind enough to commend.
>
> We have sufficient authority in the Dutch school of art, for taking as subjects of representation scenes of daily and familiar occurrence. A painter's eye will often be arrested where ordinary people see nothing remarkable. A casual gleam of sunshine, or a shadow thrown across his path, a time-withered oak, or a moss-covered stone may awaken a train of thoughts and feelings, and picturesque imaginings.

Interestingly, Talbot felt he had to make it clear that the plates were original photographs not engraved copies of photographs, 'because some well executed engravings have been published in France in imitation of Photography, but they want the character of truth and reality which that art so eminently possesses' (from a slip inserted with the first Part).

Part II was reviewed in *The Art Union* for March 1845:

> The first of these [the calotypes] is termed *The Open Door* and presents literally an open door, before which stands a broom, and near which hangs a lantern. It is, of course, an effect of sunshine, and the microscopic execution sets at nought the work of human hands. With this broom the famous broom of Wouverman* must never be compared: it becomes at once a clumsy imitation.

The journal also noted that in photography 'the minutest detail is given with a softness that cannot be imitated by any artistic manipulation'.

*Philips Wouverman, (1619–1668), Dutch painter.

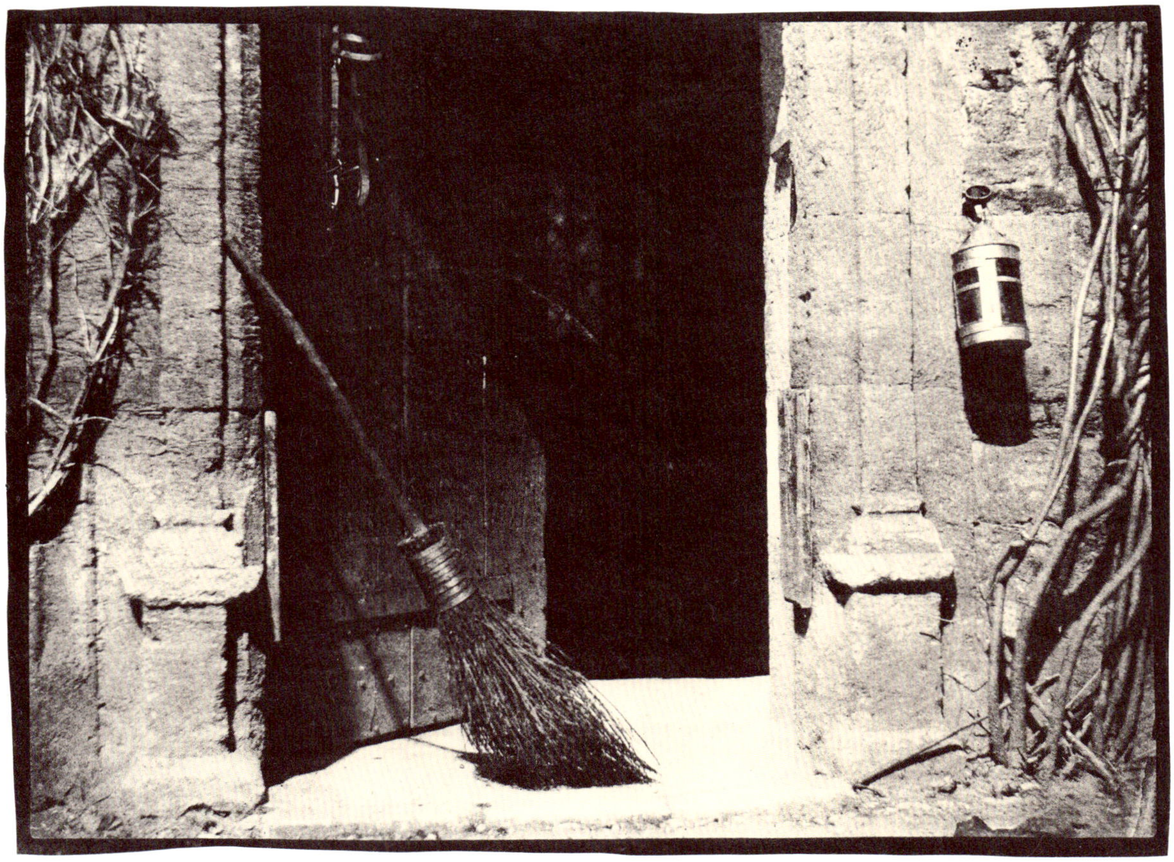

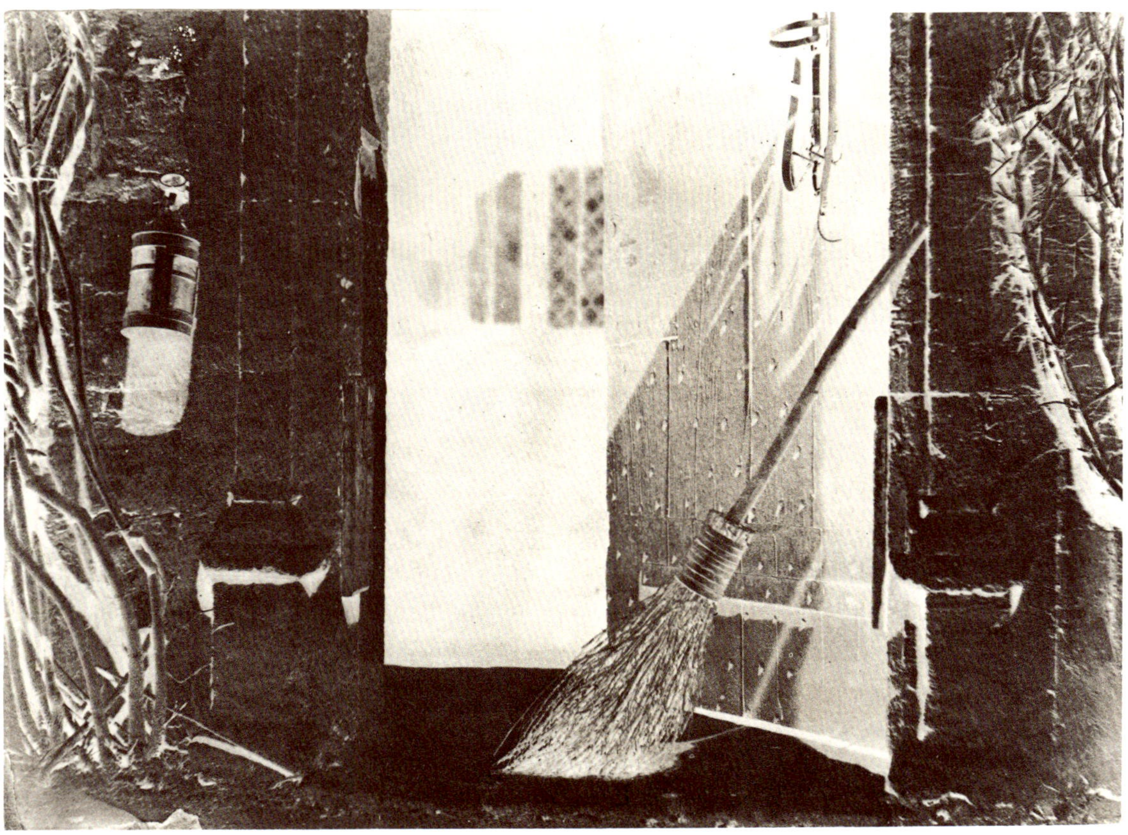

PLATE

6

Henri-Victor Regnault French 1810–78
Trees Before 1853
Developed-out salted paper print, probably from waxed paper negative
258 × 208 mm The Kodak Museum

In the first half-century of photography, the normal method for printing negatives was by printing-out. The negative was placed on a sheet of sensitised paper and held in close contact in a frame. The frame was placed in strong daylight, preferably sunlight, (hence the term sun-printing). Light passing through the negative caused the printing paper to darken directly, in proportion to the quantity of light reaching it. This process could take from many minutes to hours, depending on the negative and the strength of daylight. When the paper had reached the desired density, it was removed from the frame and fixed – chemically treated to remove the remaining silver salts to make the print permanent. This lengthy procedure limited the output of prints to a few a day from any one negative. To offset this, the photographer often made several negatives of a subject for a commercial edition of prints, which accounts for the small differences which may be seen in prints with the same subject, title and print number. L.D. Blanquart-Evrard in 1851 offered an alternative. Sensitised salted paper was exposed under a negative for a few seconds only, insufficient to form a visible image. The exposed paper was washed and then developed, in a manner similar to the negative, revealing the image. The same negative could be used to print over one hundred prints in a day, and the operation no longer depended on good daylight. While the *printed-out* image is inherently of a reddish colour, due to the very small particle size of the silver forming the image, the *developed* image on the other hand is almost completely neutral in colour, giving a black and white image. This print, from a paper negative by H.-V. Regnault, was made by Blanquart-Evrard at his establishment at Lille.

Like many other photographers of the earliest period, Regnault was a scientist: chemist, physicist, professor of the Collège de France, member of the Académie des Sciences (and from 1852 director of the Manufacture de Sèvres). When Talbot sent examples of his newly patented calotype process to the Académie in 1841 they were passed to Regnault as major specialist. This example must date before 1853 when the composition was published in *Études Photographiques*, 2nd series, printed and published by Blanquart-Evrard at Lille. The four 'studies' in the publication that are known to be by Regnault all include trees or foliage (also one of Talbot's favourite subjects). This example has an hour-glass composition. The foreground leaves are slightly out-of-focus (the sharpest focus is on the bole of the central tree); they are matched or echoed by the out-of-focus leaves on the tree, an effect caused by breeze. Trees were often chosen as a subject because, like ivy-clad ruins, they combined a variety of light and shade together with complex linear forms. This composition could be taken as an early example of the 'differential focusing' practised by P.H. Emerson (see PLATE 35). In England in 1853 the miniature painter and amateur photographer Sir William Newton publicly argued that woodland scenes thrown slightly out of focus could be more artistic than properly focused ones.

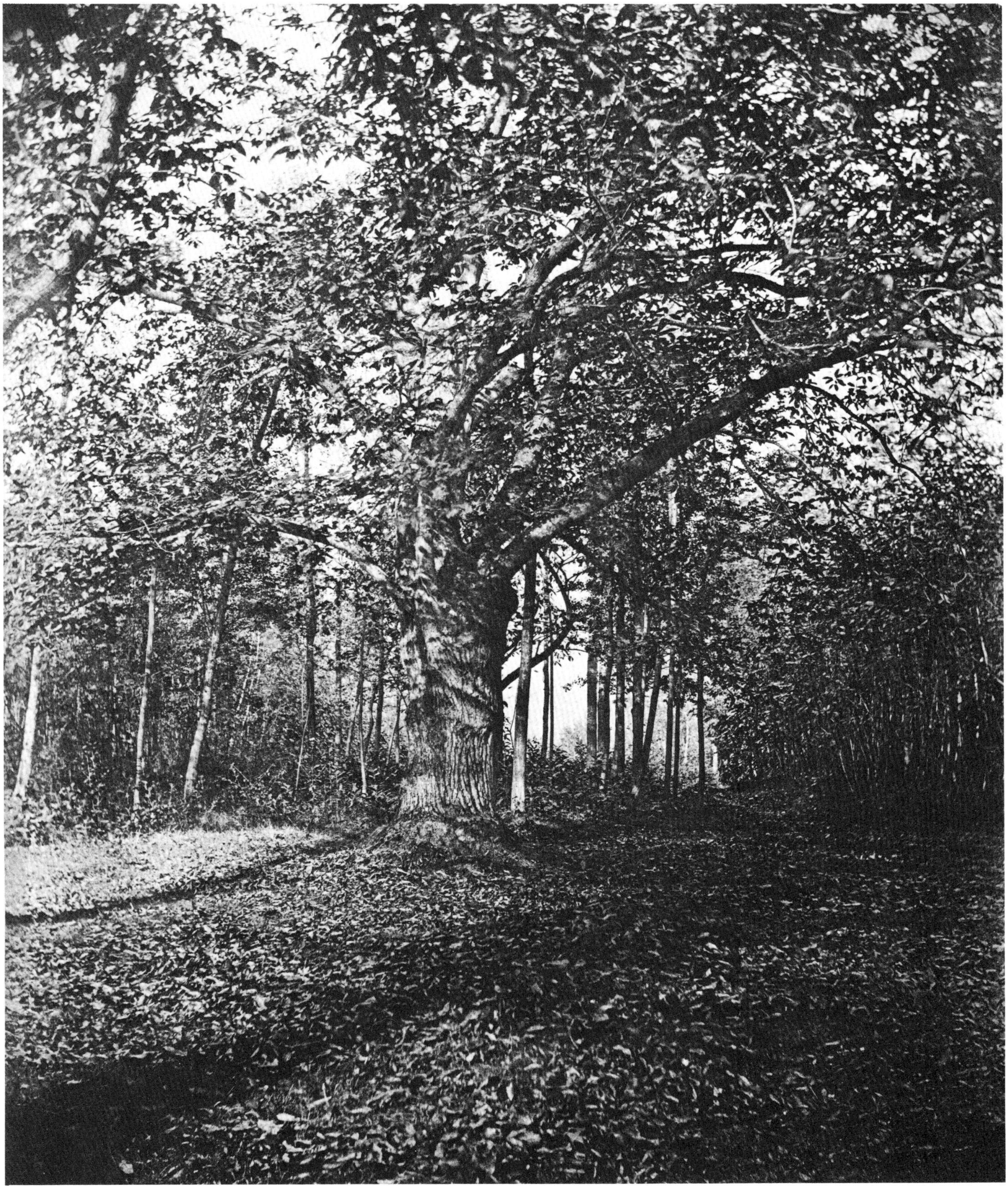

PLATE

7

John Stewart British Active 1850s
Spanish Muleteers at the Fair at Pau November 1853
Calotype, hand-tinted with watercolour, inscribed, signed and dated
173 × 120 mm (reproduced same size) The Kodak Museum

The absorbent surface of the salted paper print made colouring a much easier task than was the case with Daguerreotypes. This calotype by John Stewart was coloured with water colours, a medium ideally suited to the task as the transparent colours did not obscure the fine details of the photograph. The coated albumen paper which became the almost universally used printing material during the second half of the last century was rather less suitable for water colours, as the surface was less absorbent. Oil colours were more often used, and the opaque colours may almost completely obscure the underlying photographic image. Most photographers offered a colouring service for portraits; in the 1850s, a framed portrait might cost one guinea, with an extra 2 guineas for tinted face and hands and an extra four guineas if it was coloured throughout 'in the best style'. Photographs of paintings were sometimes offered for sale both as albumen and as salt prints (for over-painting).

Stewart was brother-in-law of Sir John Herschel, who was closely associated with Talbot's photographic discoveries and himself discovered the fixing properties of 'hypo' (without which Talbot's invention would have foundered) as well as proposing the terms 'photograph' and 'snapshot'. However, Stewart's early experiments were prompted by information passed to him by H.-V. Regnault (see PLATE 6). Stewart sent photographs by Regnault and himself to London for the first public exhibition of photographs (if we except the display which formed part of the Great Exhibition of 1851) which was arranged by the Society of Arts in 1852. Stewart collaborated with two other distinguished amateur photographers based in Pau, F. Maxwell Lyte and J.-J. Heilmann. His large salted paper prints of the Pyrenees are in the neutral tone caused by developing-out (as practised by Regnault). Herschel described them as 'among the most exquisite in their finish, and artistic in their general effect, of any specimens of that art which I have yet seen' (Catalogue, Society of Arts exhibition 1852, in which Stewart described his methods). An unattributed scene of a child with mules appears in Blanquart-Evrard's *Keepsake Photographique* and may also be by Stewart. This hand-coloured calotype continues the practice first begun when Talbot's calotypes were offered for sale in coloured versions. This example and PLATE 6 were both owned by Sir John Herschel.

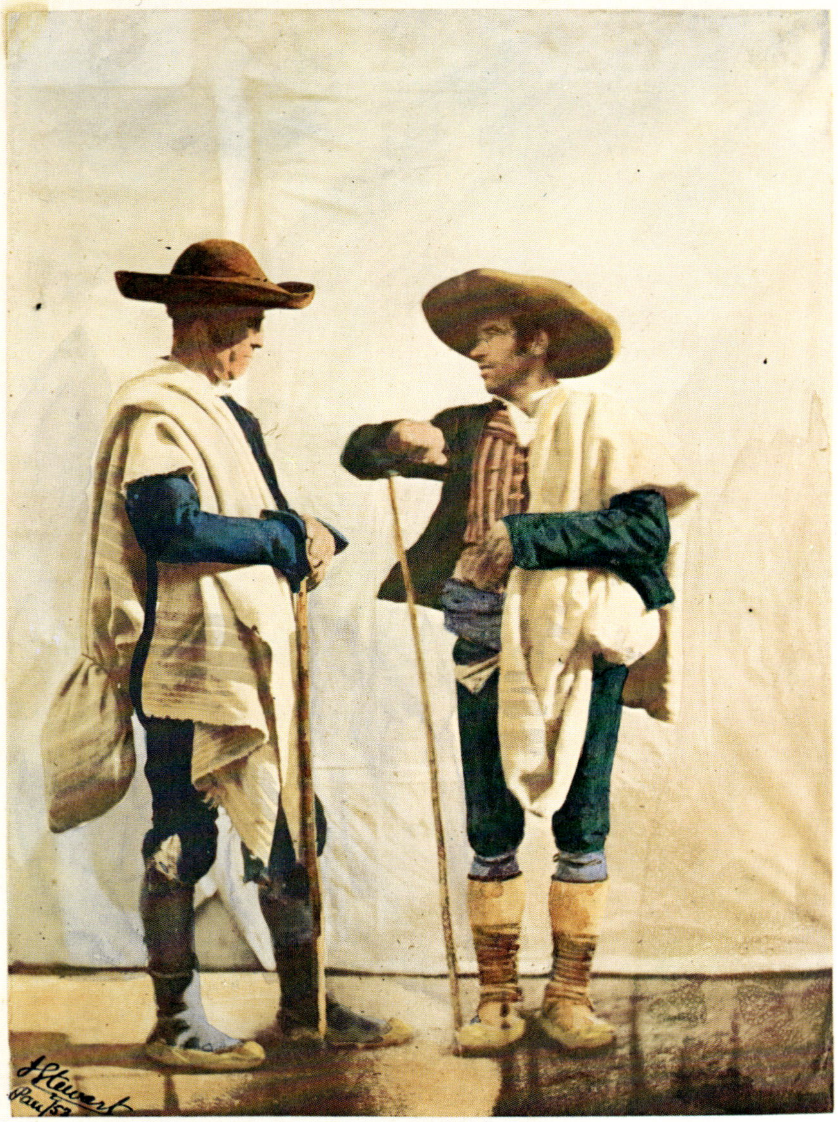

Spanish Muleteers –
– at the Fair at Pau. November 1853

PLATE

8

Gustave Le Gray French 1820–82
In the Forest of Fontainebleau 1851 (print after 1855)
Gold-toned albumen print from waxed paper negative
Facsimile signature in red ink
300 × 380 mm Mus. no. 68,007 Bequeathed by Chauncey Hare Townshend

The introduction of albumen paper by Blanquart-Evrard in 1850 coincided with the development of improved methods for making negatives with extra capacity for recording detail. Gustave Le Gray's own process, in which he waxed the calotype negative before sensitising, gave a negative with improved detail and better keeping properties. The new albumen paper, which held the image in a coating on the surface of the paper, could reproduce the finest details of the negative. As in the salted paper process, the negative was printed-out in daylight. The presence of silver in the albumen coating other than that forming the image led to a yellowing of the highlights, or white, of the picture through reaction with sulphur compounds in the atmosphere and in the paper, and this yellowing is a useful method of distinguishing between a very lightly coated albumen paper and a salted paper print, where no yellowing will be present normally. In this print by Le Gray, the image has been partially gold-toned, changing the image colour from the normal reddish-brown to a purplish-brown.

Le Gray trained in the studios of Picot and Paul Delaroche and became the inspiration and teacher of many of the generation which took up the art of photography in the 1850s, including Nadar. He made an extensive series of views in the Forest of Fontainebleau using his new process in 1851. Early salted paper prints from these negatives are a sombre, bronze colour. In about 1855 he reprinted some of the negatives on albumen paper to achieve a warmer and more golden print colour as in this example. This print and others from the series were bought by one of the earliest identifiable collectors (aside from the Royal Family) of fine photographs, the Reverend Chauncey Hare Townshend. Townshend also acquired the work of the Barbizon painter Henri Rousseau. In general terms the waxed paper process allowed crisper detail but longer exposure times than the calotype; here because of the longer exposure time the foliage outlines are softened by movement in the breeze. The atmospheric shimmer of the foliage in these prints appears to be unparalleled in other photographs of the time. Le Gray could be described as the major photographer of the Barbizon School.

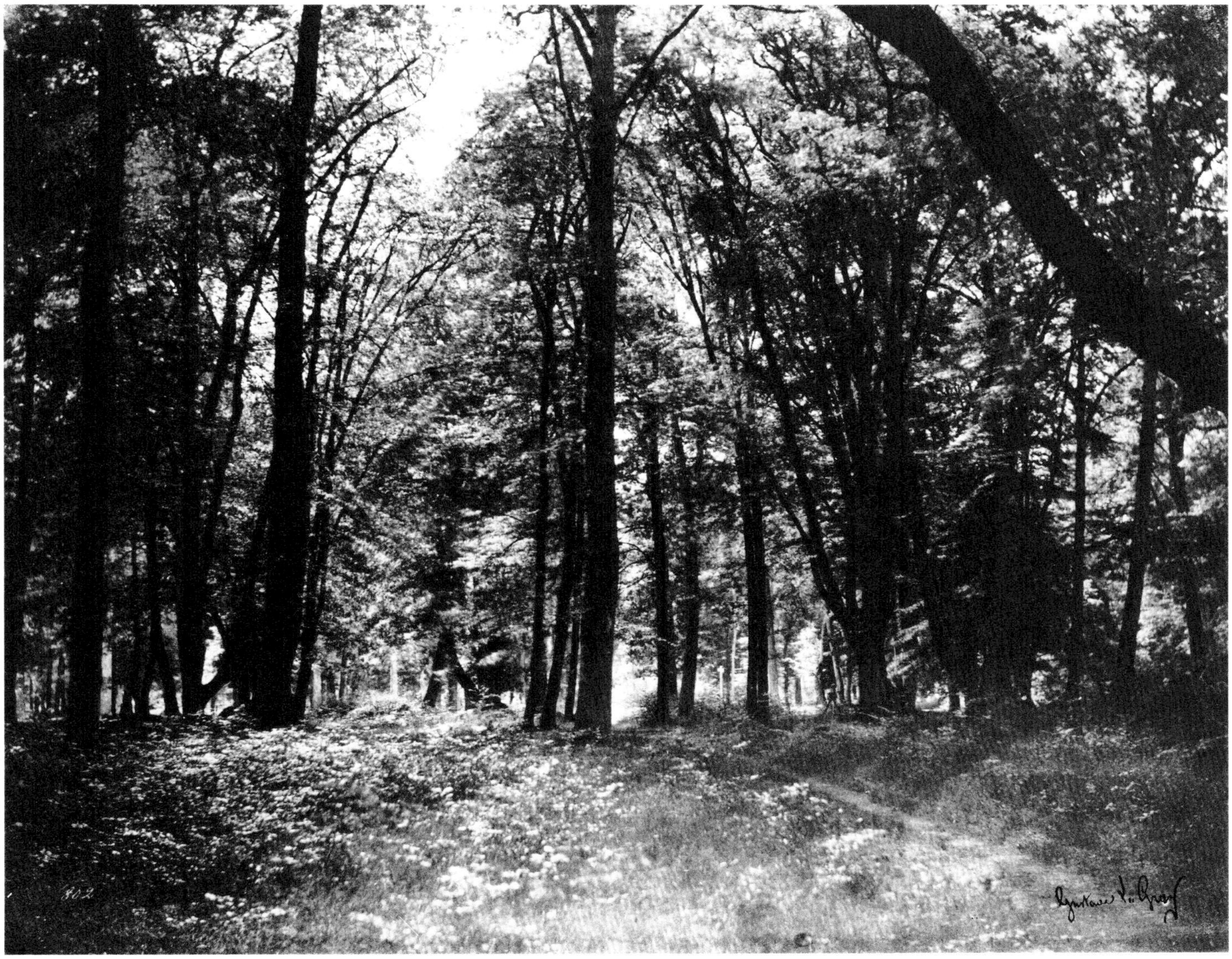

PLATE

9

Samuel Smith British circa 1801–92
The River Nene. Looking downstream. Wisbech 1861
Albumen print and the original waxed paper negative
Image size 208 × 256 mm The Kodak Museum

The negative, made translucent by waxing, shows the typical white crease marks made when the wax film is broken by flexing the paper. The photographer's annotations appear on the margins of the negative including the exposure time of 15 minutes. When exposure times were long it was usual, as here, to photograph ships at low tide. With the ships grounded there would be no movement to blur the fine detail of rigging and masts. The albumen print was one of the series probably made by Smith for public display to illustrate a report on the state of the river and proposals for a new dock.

He began photography in 1852, a year after publication by Le Gray of the waxed paper process. Although Le Gray himself later adopted the new collodion on glass process (PLATE 11) Samuel Smith continued with the earlier and slower method until he gave up photography in 1864. He is in many ways typical of the amateurs who took up the medium in the 1850s. He was the son of a farmer but was able to retire from business before he was 50 and devote himself to a variety of pursuits – astronomy, geology, palaeontology, the study of gems, coins and shells and the flora and fauna of the Fens. He was much associated with the town museum at Wisbech where many of his negatives and prints are preserved. His oeuvre of 400 photographs is almost entirely devoted to his local townscape and church architecture.

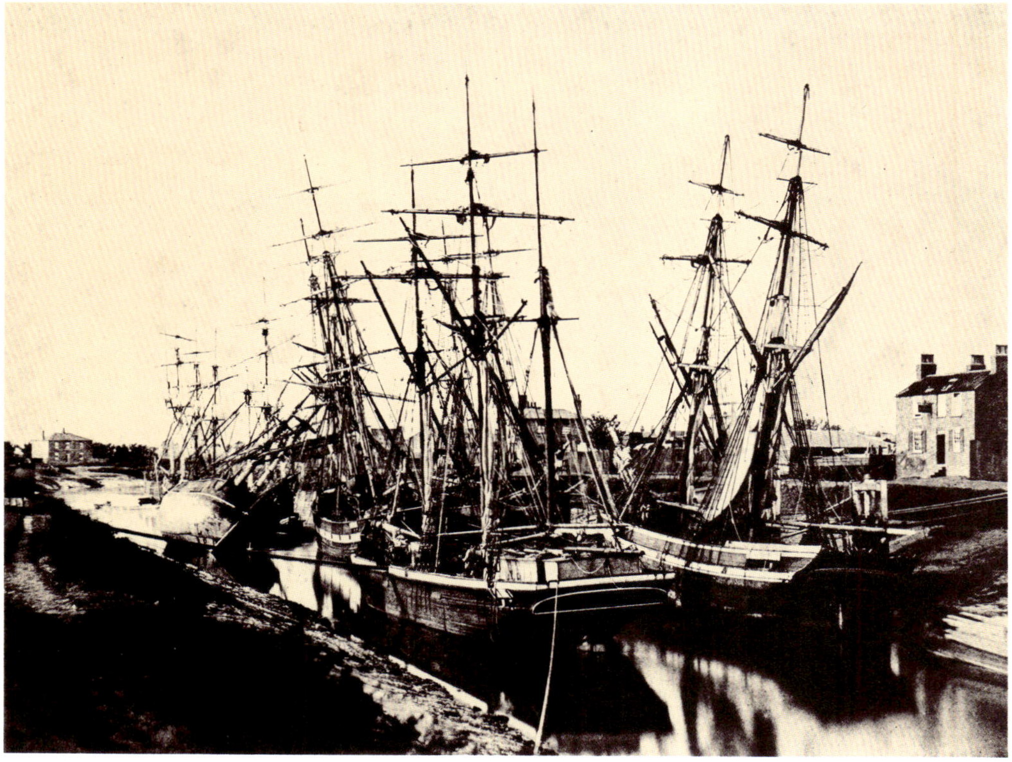

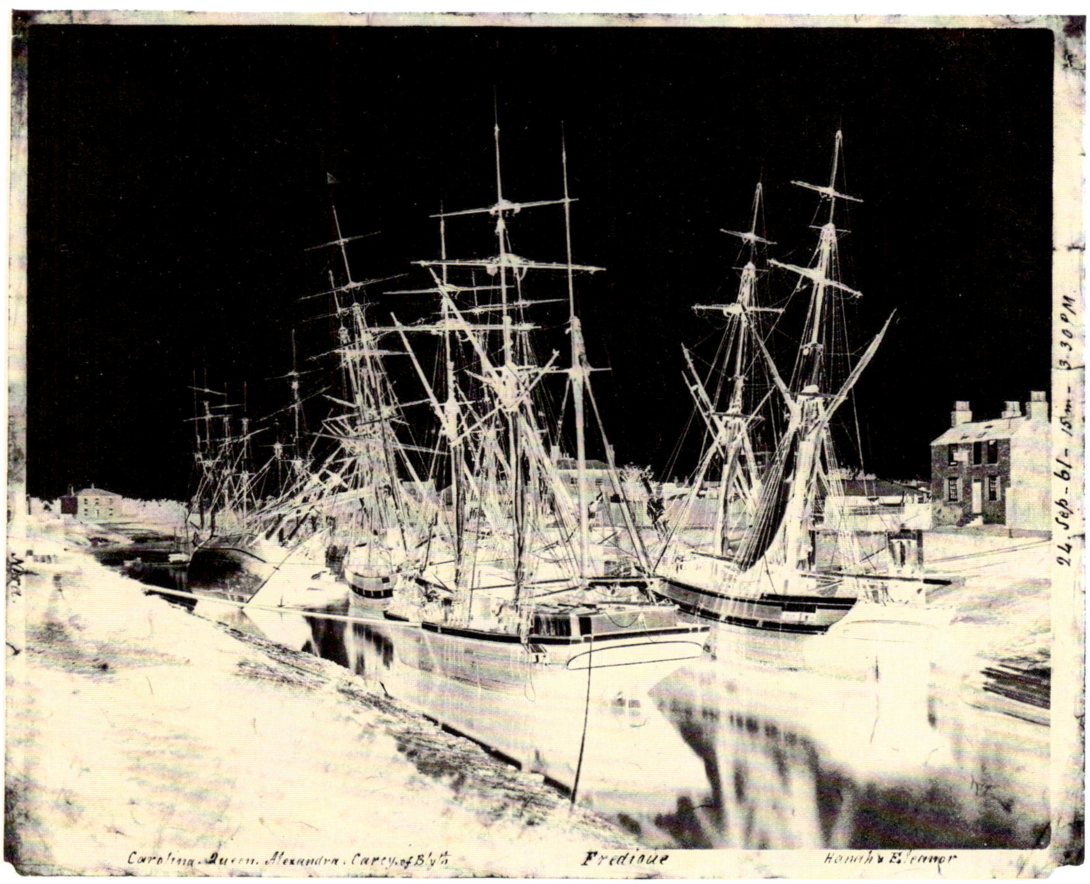
24. Sep-61- 15m- 3.30PM.
Carolina. Queen. Alexandra. Carey. of Blyth
Fredique
Hannah & Eleanor

PLATE

10

Roger Fenton British 1819–69
Balaklava from Guards Hill, the Crimea 1855
Albumen print from wet collodion negative
280 × 345 mm Mus. no. 64,854 Bequeathed by Chauncey Hare Townshend
Mount engraved with title and: 'Photographed by R. Fenton. Manchester, Published by T. Agnew & Sons, Nov 19th 1855, London, P. & D. Colnaghi & Co. Paris, Moulin 23 Rue Richer. New York, Williams & Co.'

This albumen print by Fenton is so lightly coated that on superficial examination it might pass for a salted paper print. However, the faint but discernible sheen on the paper surface, and the yellowed highlights, reveal its true nature. The reddish-brown image shows no obvious sign of gold toning, which although widely used for albumen prints was not universally employed, contrary to the impression given in some recent writings. All the early negative processes were sensitive only to blue light, and white clouds and blue sky recorded much more strongly on the plate than did the landscape. In prints from early negatives, the skies tend to be featureless, unless specially prepared cloud negatives were used in a double printing operation to add an attractive sky. To facilitate this, and to remove coating imperfections which would be all too apparent in a large area free of detail, it was often the practice to paint out the sky area on the negative with opaque medium. There are clear signs along the skyline of this photograph that it was done in this case.

Like Gustave Le Gray, Roger Fenton trained as a painter in the studio of Delaroche, and like his French contemporary, Fenton represents the highest aspirations of the art of photography in his time. Neither adapted to the era of mass production in photography which developed from about 1860. Fenton excelled in all of the medium's fields but his documentation of the Crimean War, commissioned by Thomas Agnew & Sons and assisted by Royal patronage, remains his most-published work. His photographs are the first convincing document of a theatre of war. He worked in the Crimea with a mobile darkroom (a specially designed horse-drawn van) and two assistants. The glass negatives were sensitized with collodion solution in the van and exposed while still wet, then immediately developed in the van. This view successfully delineates the anchorage at Balaklava and the surrounding terrain, complete with the aerial perspective intrinsic to photography. Unlike most of Fenton's photographs there are minor technical flaws (fogging of the negative in three places – not to be confused with the smoke or steam rising from one of the ships) but these do not seriously affect the value of the view.

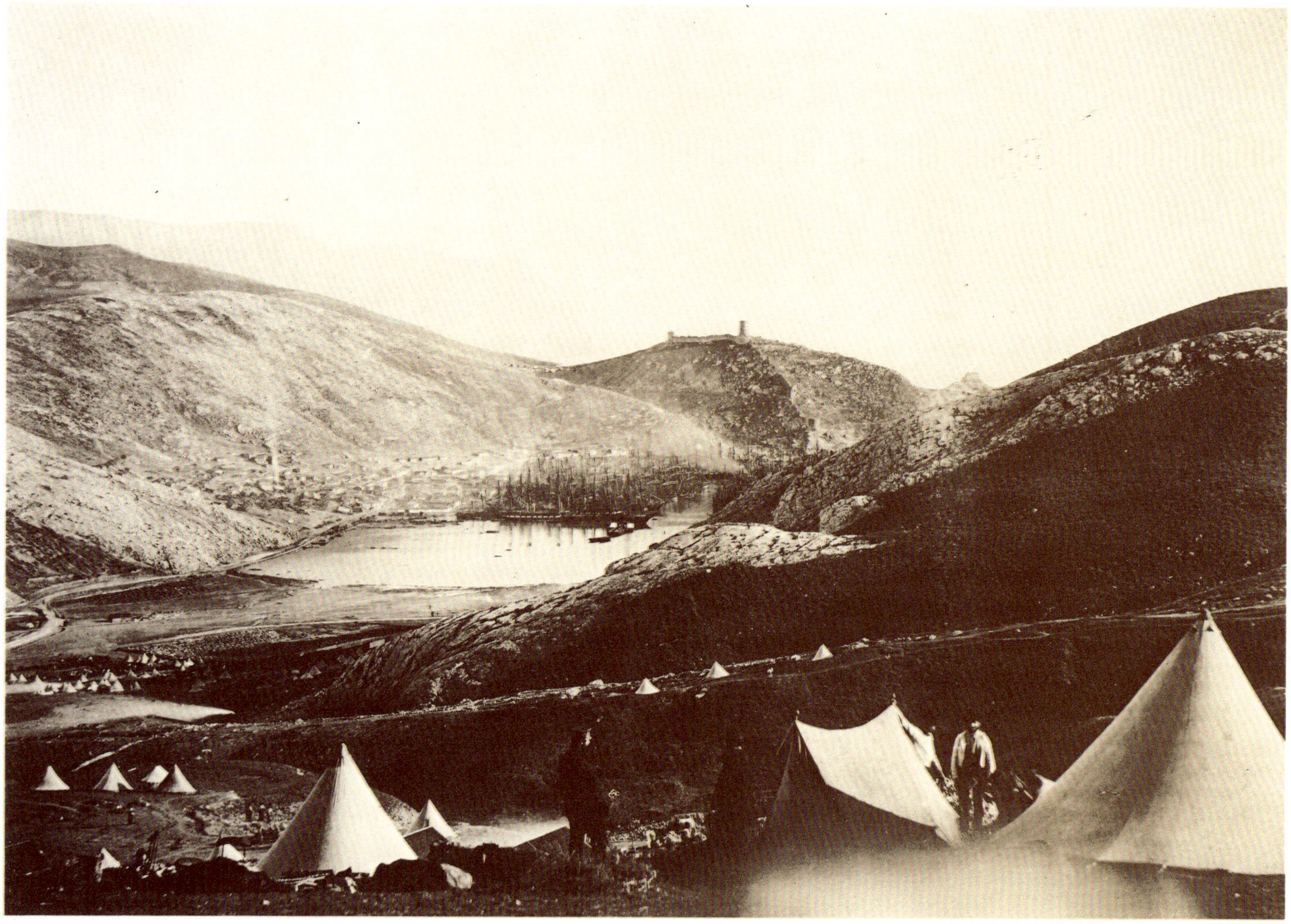

PLATE

11

Gustave Le Gray French 1820–82
The imperial yacht 'La Reine Hortense' at Le Havre 1856
Gold toned albumen print from wet collodion negative
Facsimile signature in red ink
323 × 415 mm Mus. no. 68,006 Bequeathed by Chauncey Hare Townshend

Gustave Le Gray's striking record of the Imperial yacht shows an effective combination of the high resolution wet collodion negative and the albumen printing paper, giving a finely detailed print. The 15 minutes needed by Samuel Smith for his river scene (PLATE 9) were not necessary here, as the wet collodion process was appreciably faster, but the blurring of some of the quay-side figures – some are mere 'ghosts' – indicates that the exposure still ran to many seconds. The print shows the typical yellowed highlights of the albumen print, partially gold-toned.

Le Gray undertook commissions for the Emperor of France. The steam yacht was named after the Emperor's mother and was much used for Imperial tours and visits following the conclusion of the Crimean War and the Universal Exhibition of 1855 (at which Le Gray was awarded the highest medal for photography). This view of the Imperial yacht was perhaps taken prior to its departure, bearing Prince Napoleon, on an expedition to Greenland and Spitzbergen in June 1856. The tallest figure on deck, apparently smiling, has been identified as the Prince himself. The figures would have been posed for the picture, which must have been taken from one of the escort vessels of the expedition. During the same summer Le Gray made his instantaneous photographs of the sea, which provided one of the photographic sensations of the decade. The print indicates Le Gray's mastery of the wet collodion process and forms a comparison to the atmospheric effects he achieved with the waxed paper process (PLATE 8).

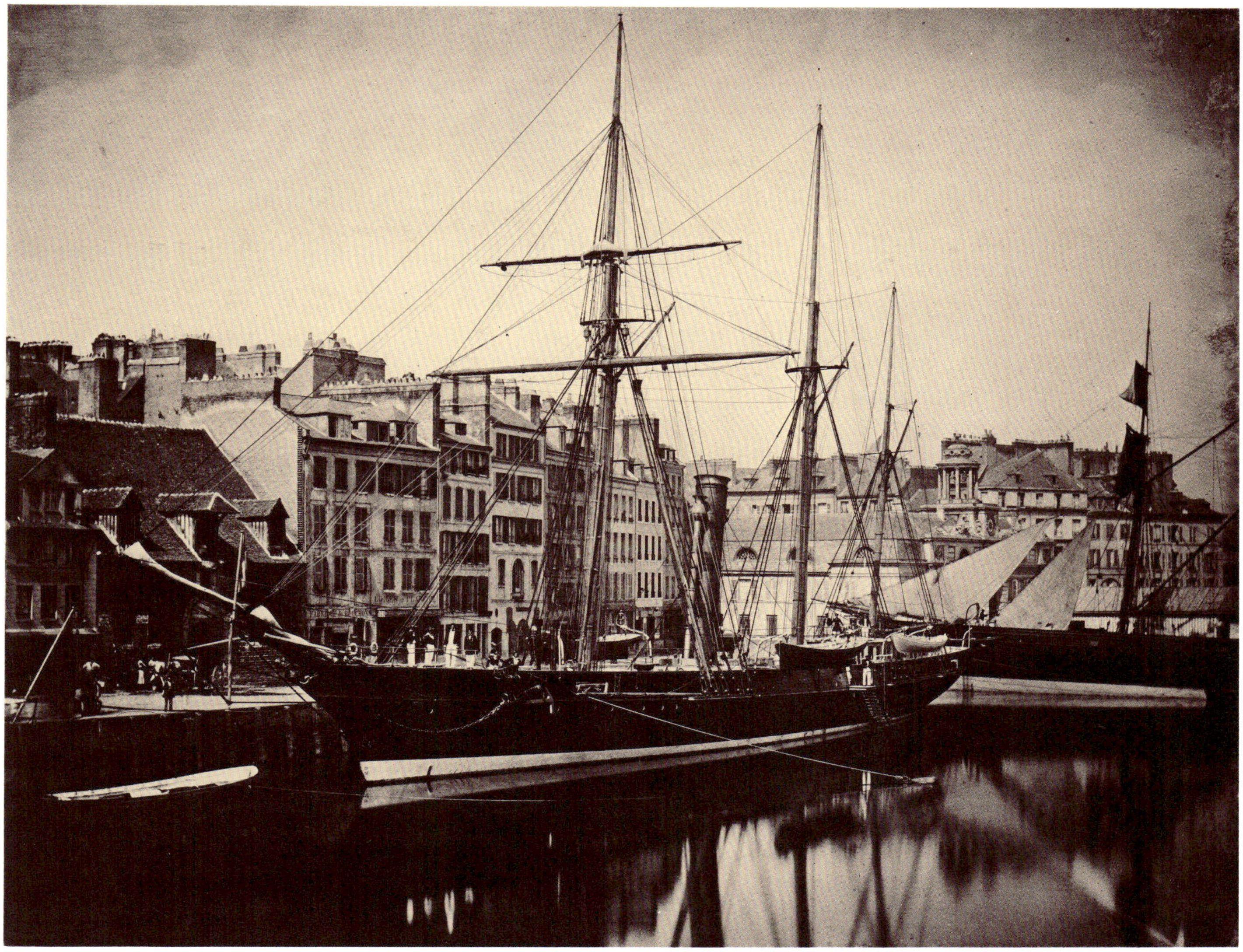

PLATE

12

Camille Silvy French born 1835, active circa 1858–68
River Scene, France 1858
Gold-toned albumen print from two wet collodion negatives
Signed in red ink on the mount
245 × 370 mm Mus. no. 68,012 Bequeathed by Chauncey Hare Townshend

Camille Silvy's remarkable landscape has been heavily printed, to a level which in an ordinary photograph would have produced muddied tones. Here the combination of lighting and subject has held the over-printing well, and the subsequent gold toning has added to the richness of the print. The movement of ducks across the river suggests an exposure time of ten seconds or more. This is one of the best documented, most aesthetically impressive and technically interesting of early photographs – and also most rare (only a somewhat faded copy in the Société Française de Photographie is known, apart from this mint example). It was first exhibited at the Photographic Society of Scotland, Edinburgh, in 1858. A critic wrote:

> Perhaps the gem of the whole exhibition is (582) 'River Scene – France' by C. Silvy. We have seen no photograph which has taken our fancy so much as that exhibited under this unpretending title by Messrs Murray & Heath [London photographers, suppliers, print publishers]. The natural beauty of the scene itself, rich in exquisite and varied detail, with the broad, soft shadows stealing over the whole, produce a picture which for calm, inviting beauty we have not seen equalled. (*Journal of the Photographic Society*, 5 February 1859)

Early negatives could not deal with the brightness range of a relatively bright (blue) sky and darker toned (green) earth. Silvy combined separately exposed negatives – possibly made consecutively at the same scene – to make this print. Like other photographers, he selectively masked and 'dodged' local areas (most noticeable round the rooftop at left) and 'burned in' the foreground to balance the sky. The site is the river Huisne west of Chartres at Nogent-le-Rotrou. The photograph was also shown at the Salon de Photographie of 1859 in Paris, an exhibition famous among other things for provoking Baudelaire's eloquent outburst against the art pretentions of photography which he linked to the claims of Naturalism.

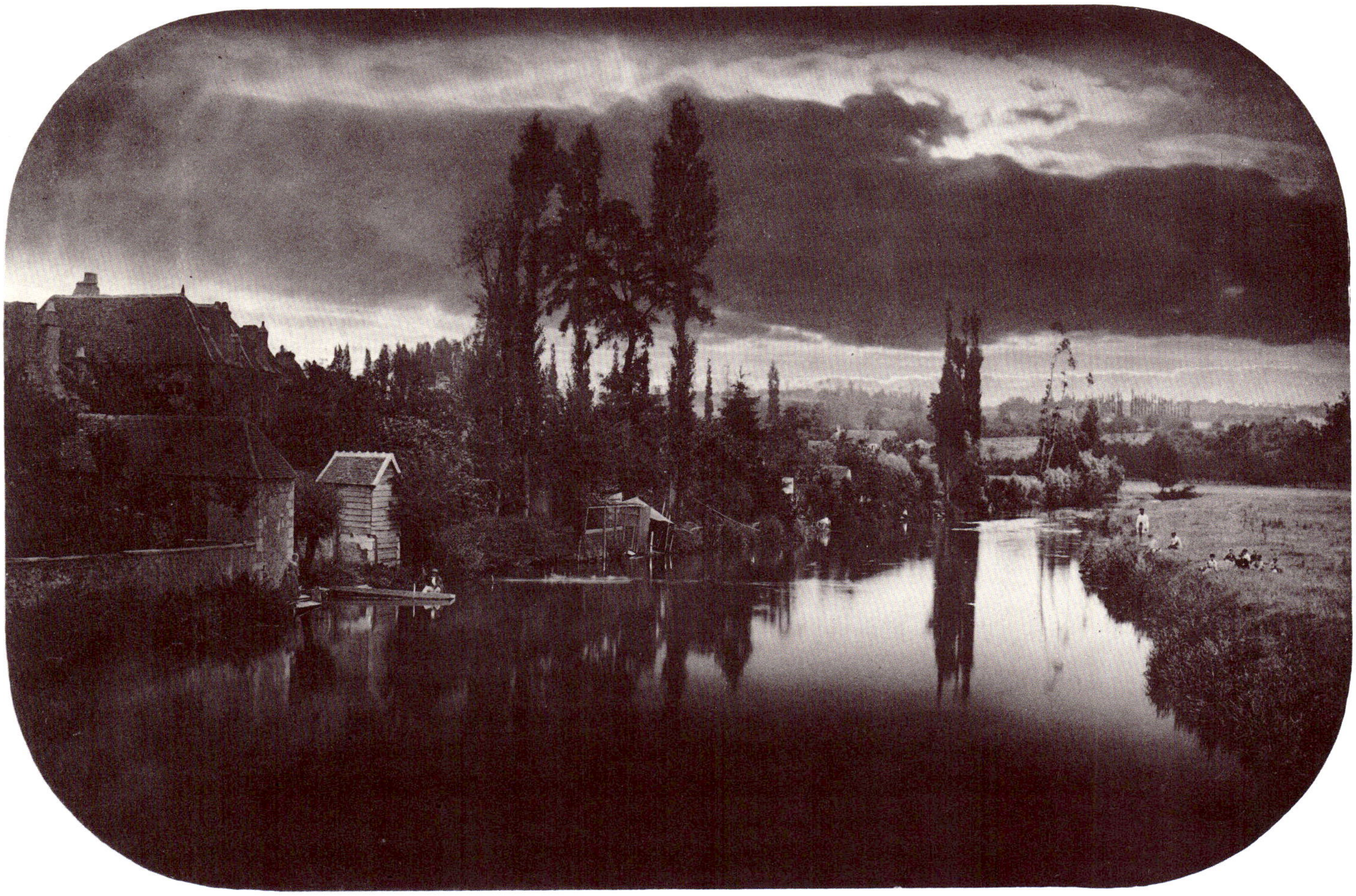

C. Silvy

PLATE

13

Julia Margaret Cameron British 1815–79
Circe 1864–65
Gold toned albumen print from wet collodion negative
Signed, titled and inscribed by the photographer on the mount:
'From Life Circe "Who knows not Circe/Daughter of the Sun"'
P & D Colnaghi stamp on mount, lettered 'Registered Photograph'
244 × 202 mm Mus. no. 45,140 Given by the photographer

Mrs Cameron's technical skills as a photographer were more limited than her imagination and many of her photographs are effective in spite of their imperfections. The limited depth of field of her portrait lens used at full aperture, and the long exposure times, combine to produce a softness of detail unusual for the period – although it was to become a fashion at the end of the century with the rise of 'impressionist' photography. Many of her photographs, including this one, show a crêpe-like pattern in the image; this almost certainly results from too thick a coating of collodion on her plate. This is a case, perhaps, in which her imperfect techniques contributed by happy accident to the effect of the final result. Very large numbers of mounted copies of her photographs were sold or distributed, either printed on albumen paper – as in this example – or by the carbon process (see PLATE 30).

Mrs Cameron's career began with the gift of a wet collodion camera and darkroom equipment from her daughter and son-in-law in 1863. Her portraits boldly revived a tradition of artistic imprecision in photography (see PLATES 6 and 8) and carried it to an extreme of expressive intent. Her hall-mark is the extreme close-up thrown slightly out of focus. Her methods veiled detail by optical means (rather than by re-touching, which spoils much portrait photography of the later collodion era). In the 1850s and early 1860s some photographers, notably Claudet, had sought means of softening the ultra-sharp and often unflattering delineation of physiognomy which was thought of as a problematic feature of the collodion process. Mrs Cameron's intentions were clearly to draw from her sitters ideal, symbolic or universal qualities. In this photograph the title invites us to find in a young girl (Kate Keown, born in 1857) the imprint of the sorceress daughter of the sun, preparer of the magic cup whose contents changed the companions of Odysseus into swine. Characteristic of many of Mrs Cameron's portraits is the dark background from which the head emerges, lit by diffused light (although, of course, some of her major portraits are lit starkly and dramatically).

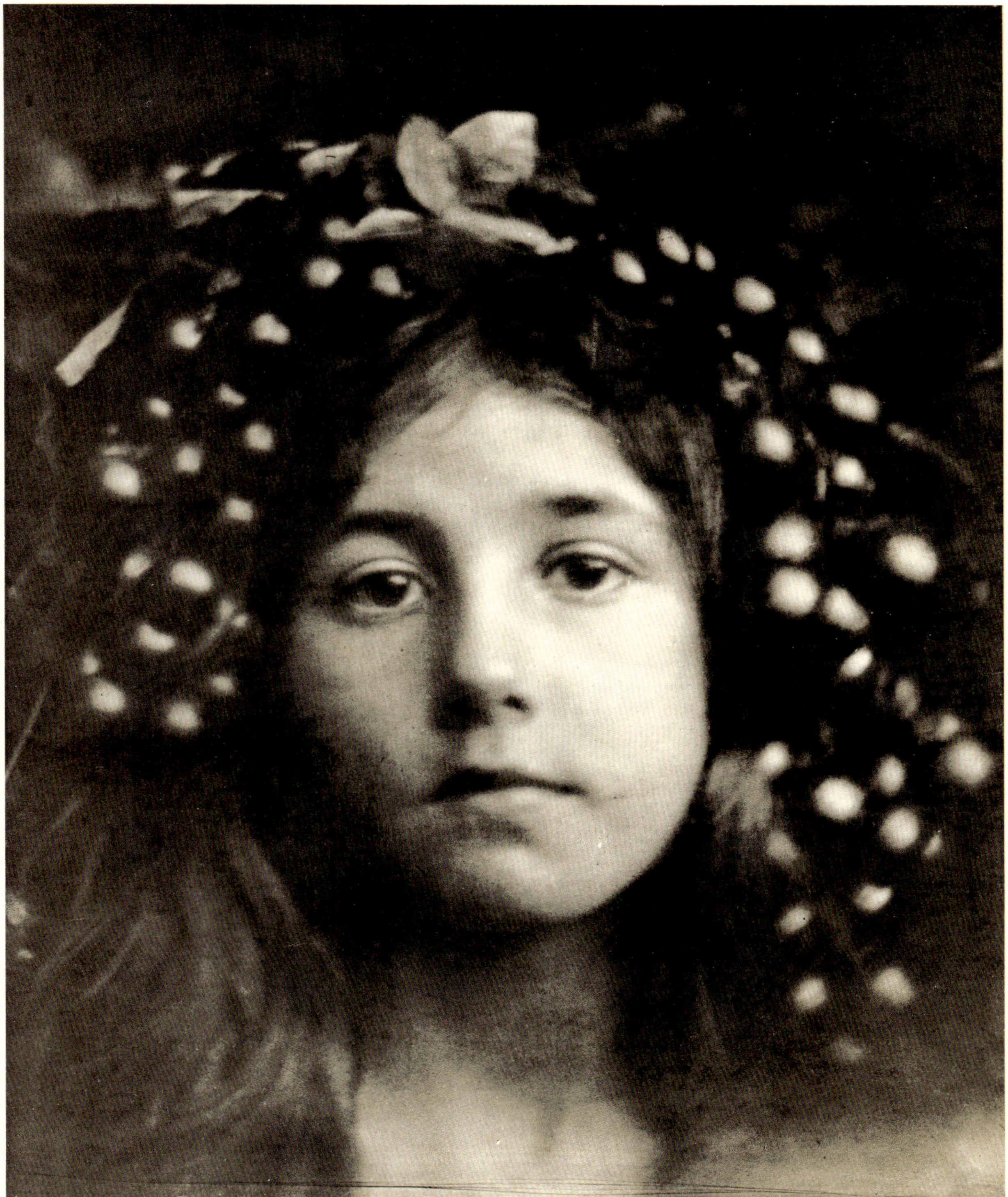

From Life — Julia Margaret Cameron

Circe

"Who knows not Circe"
"Daughter of the Sun"

PLATE

14

Clementina, Viscountess Hawarden British 1822–65
Photographic study early 1860s
Albumen print from wet collodion negative
236 × 268 mm Mus. no. 324–1948 Given by Lady Clementina Tottenham

Lady Hawarden's photographs are often remarkable for their lighting, and this is no exception. Unlike Mrs Cameron, who so often used diffused, rather flat lighting, Lady Hawarden has here made use of strong sunlight falling on her sitter from a window. Such circumstances normally lead to an intolerably wide range of contrast between highlight and shadow. The shadow side of the sitter's face is lit by reflected light from the table-top, and this 'fill-in' lighting has kept the contrast within acceptable limits. The albumen print has not been gold toned, and shows the consequently very yellowed highlights.

The title of this photograph is the one used by the photographer in the catalogues of the exhibitions in which she showed in her lifetime. Her mentor in photography appears to have been the High Art photographer Oscar Rejlander, who wrote after her death: 'She was an earnest believer in the progress of photography, and that it could be used as an art and abused like a daub. She worked honestly, in a good, comprehensible style. She aimed at elegant and, if possible, idealised truth' (*The British Journal of Photography*, 27 January 1865). Lady Hawarden belongs, like Mrs Cameron, to the second wave of amateur photographers – which emerged when the technological problems of the albumen/collodion combination had been solved and materials more or less standardized. Her work received critical praise (including that of Lewis Carroll). Her photographs are mostly figure compositions taken in her photography room on the first floor of her house in Prince's Gate, South Kensington. This photograph demonstrates her interest in bold lighting effects of a kind impermissible in professional portrait photography of the period, arrangements of pattern, and luxurious costume. Her models were her three daughters and son.

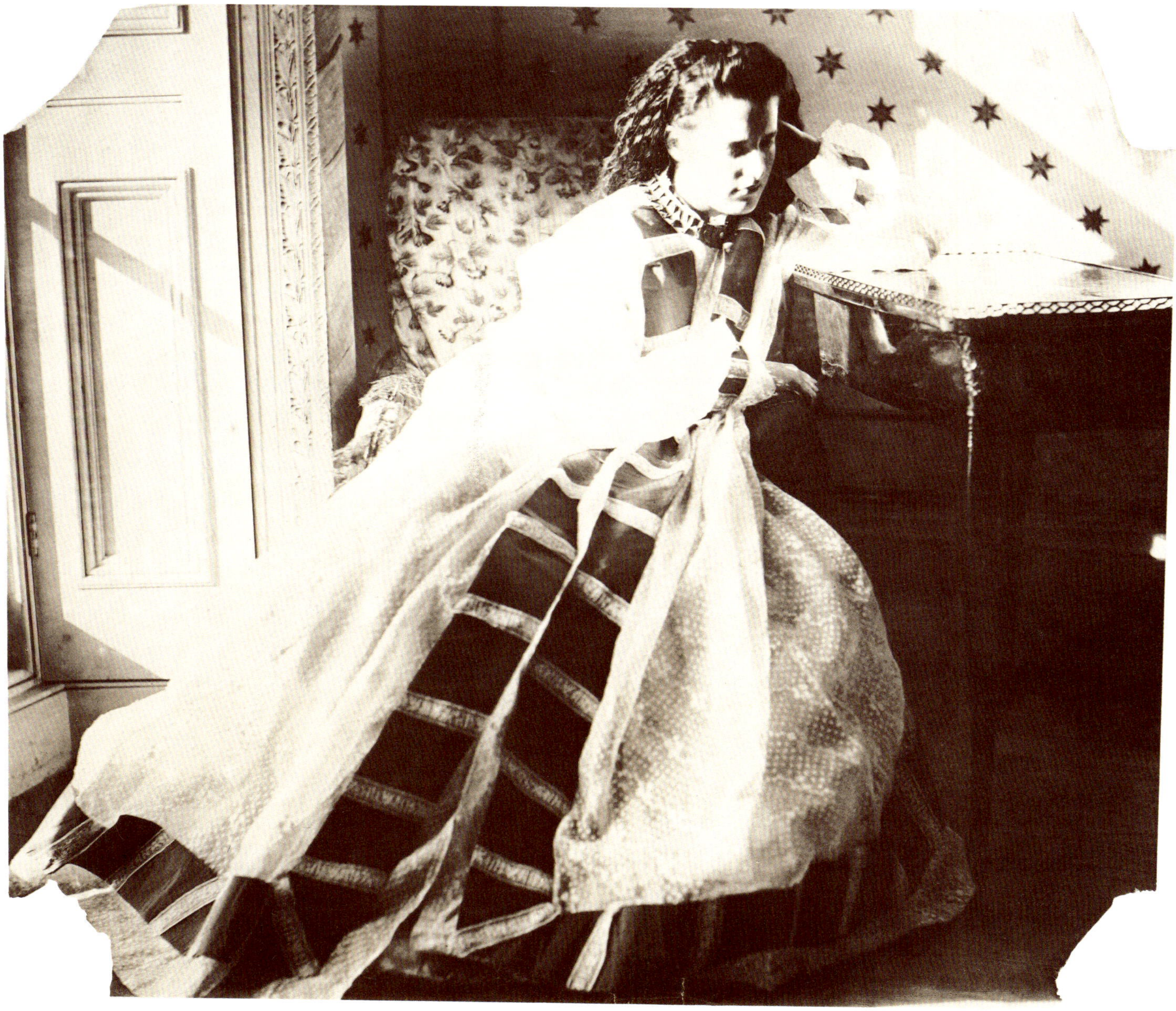

PLATE

15

Camille Silvy French, born 1835 (active 1858–68)
Portrait of a lady Early 1860s
Gold-toned albumen print from wet collodion negative
85 × 56 mm (reproduced same size)

This format was christened the *carte de visite,* apparently with the notion that the common visiting card should carry a photograph of its owner. The name has stuck and *cartes* are the most plentiful surviving form of 19th century photograph. The most stylish master of this mass-produced imagery was Silvy (see also PLATE 12) and this example is from his famous series *The Beauties of England* (a photographic continuation of a genre earlier established in engravings). The craze for *carte* collecting began about 1860. Despite the name these pictures were not used as visiting cards but they were exchanged among friends and assembled into albums.

Bourne and Shepherd studio founded 1861
Portrait of a man in fancy dress Date unknown
137 × 97 mm Mus. No. 372–1956 Provenance unknown

The 'Cabinet' format was a portrait size which was effectively introduced by the London portrait photographers Window and Bridge in 1866 and taken up as a new stimulus to business after the *carte* collecting craze had waned. The standard size was a photograph of 140 × 102mm on a card of 165 × 108mm, although some studios preferred a shorter length as in this example – which could have been taken in Bourne and Shepherd's studios in Simla, Bombay or Calcutta. Like the carte, the cabinet portrait remained popular until the First World War.

Anonymous photographer
Marvels of the Stereoscope – What is seen and what is not seen About 1860
Albumen print from wet collodion negative, hand painted
Each frame: 75 × 68 mm, mounted on card 85 × 175 mm (reproduced same size)
Inscribed on reverse: 'E.T./*73*'

Stereoscopic photographs provide the third popular format in which albumen photographs are found. The genre owes its introduction to the inventions of Wheatstone (1838) and Brewster (1849). The display of stereoscopic Daguerreotypes by Duboscq at the Great Exhibition aroused the admiration of Queen Victoria and stereoscopic photography soon achieved widespread popularity. Its illusion of three-dimensionality encourages the 'mesmerised' viewing satirised in this characteristically playful example. The London Stereoscopic Co emblazoned its catalogue of '10,000 Groups and Scenes, from Nature's loveliest nook and dell to its grandest alpine glacier' with this quotation: 'Seems madam! Nay it IS!' (*Hamlet*).

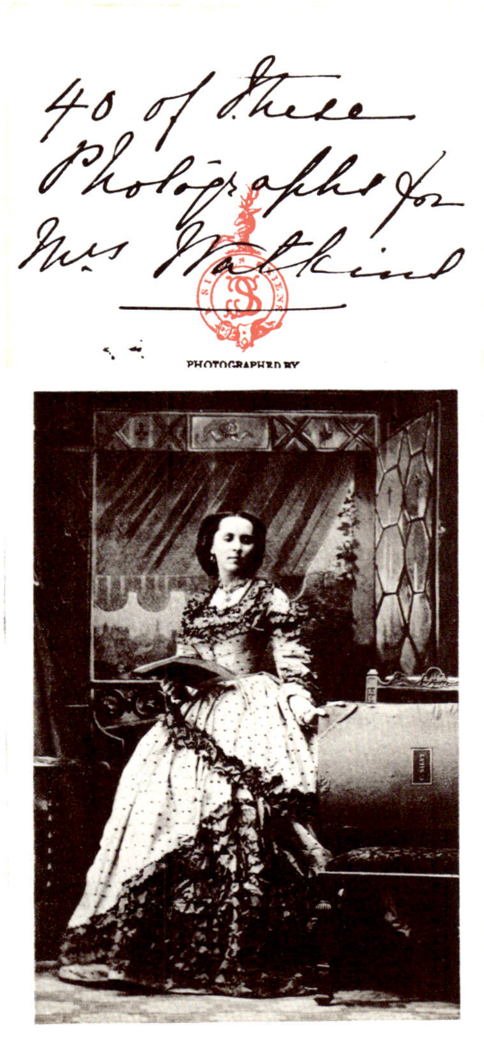
40 of these
Photographs for
Mrs Watkins
PHOTOGRAPHED BY

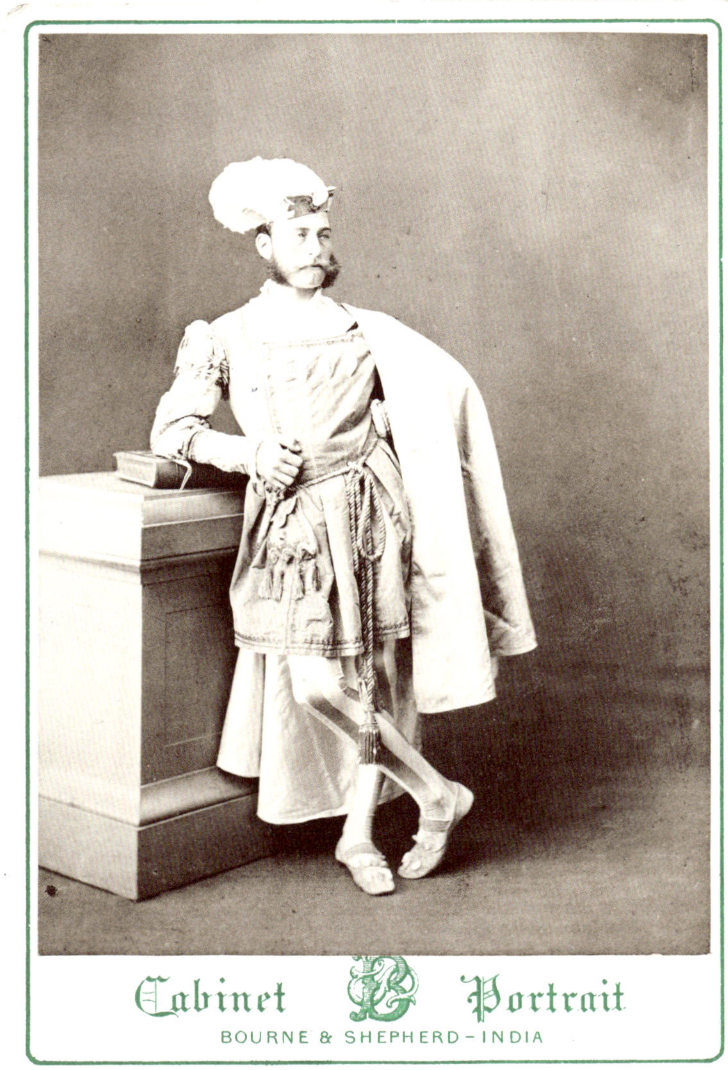
Cabinet Portrait
BOURNE & SHEPHERD - INDIA

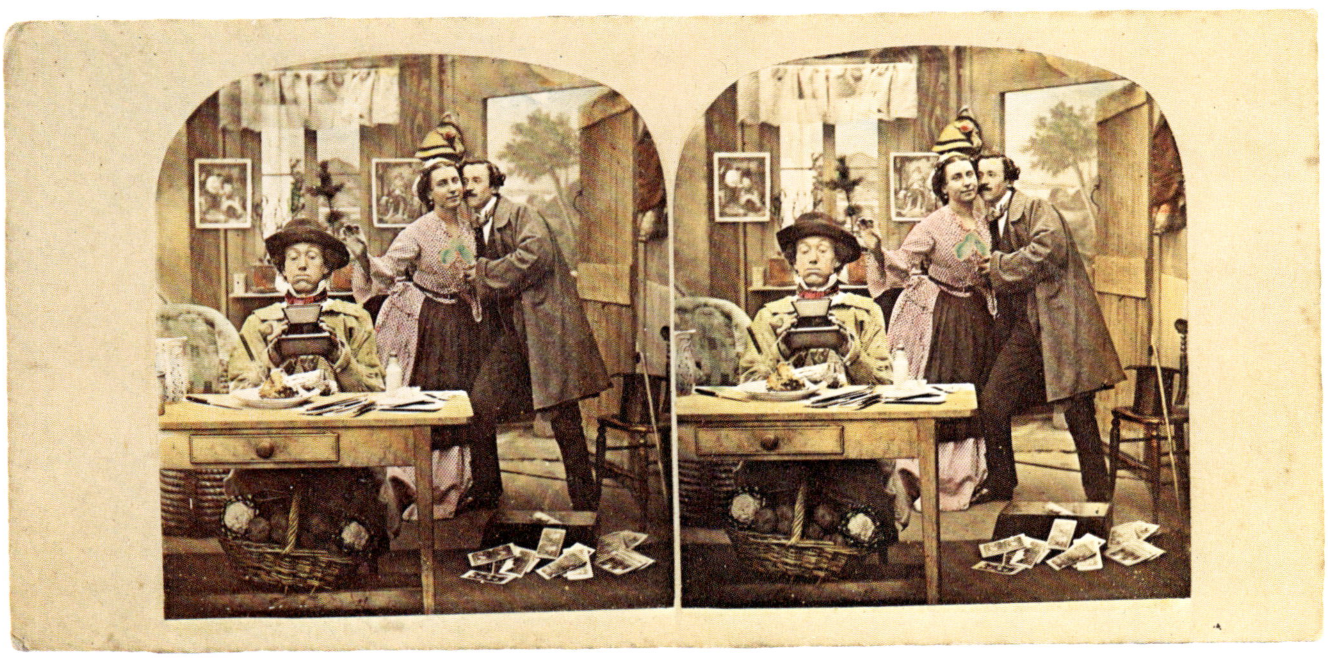

PLATE

16

George Davison British 1854–1930
A Rural Scene About 1887
Gelatin-silver chloride printing-out paper; toned and untoned examples
231 × 183mm and 235 × 183mm The Kodak Museum

George Davison (see PLATE 17) became the leading exponent of photographic impressionism, after the success of his soft-focus picture 'An Old Farmstead', taken with a pinhole camera, which won the gold medal at the Photographic Society exhibition in 1890. His photographs, and his theories on impressionism in photography, had a great influence on his contemporaries. His work spans the change in photography at the end of the last century, when the new materials, faster and more convenient than the old wet collodion process, liberated photographers from a necessary preoccupation with the technicalities of the process and allowed freer expression and easier experimentation. The old school, the 'f/64' photographers, used small lens apertures (and consequently long exposures) so that every detail was sharply recorded. The new materials, much faster and easier to use, permitted short exposures with hand held cameras, and photographers discovered the virtues of selective focusing. Davison's early naturalistic photography owed much to the old traditions; this pair of examples, from *c*1887, was taken with a 10 × 8 inch stand camera; the slight blurring in the trees shows the exposure to have been a second or two. The disposition of the figures might seem to be chance; comparison of the two pictures shows small differences – the position of the dog and the turn of the head of the woman at the pump. They had been carefully posed, and asked to hold the pose for at least two time exposures. The prints were made on a gelatin-silver chloride printing-out paper; one has not been gold toned, and shows a grey-brown image colour and has faded to some extent. The other, with the characteristic purplish colour of gold toning, has not suffered in the same way.

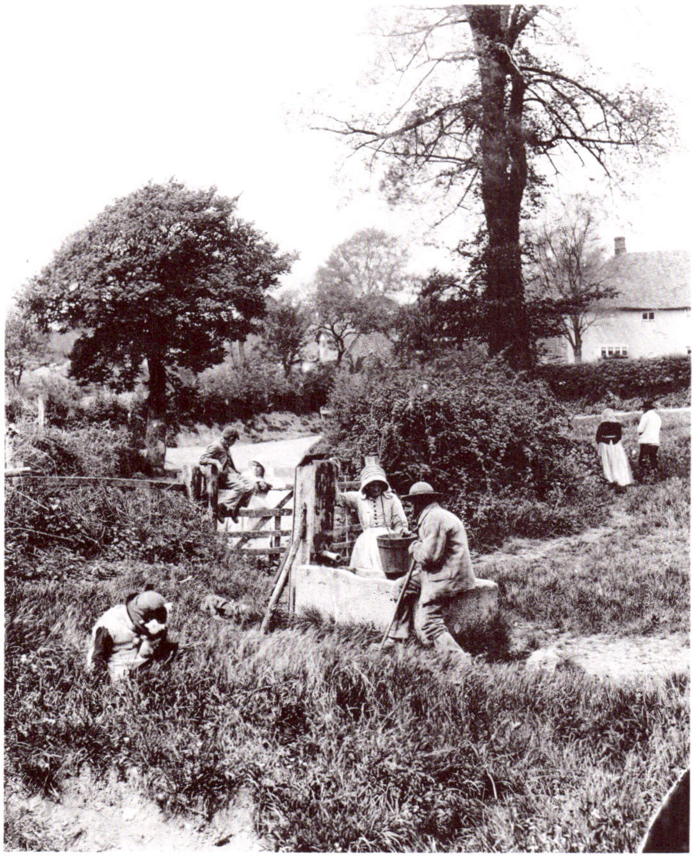

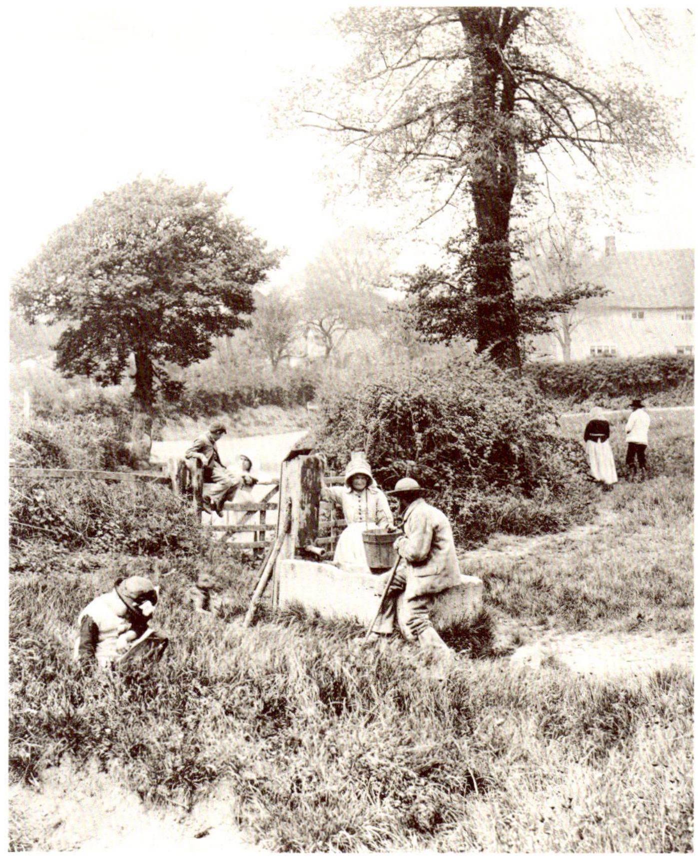

PLATE

17

George Davison British 1854–1930
From the series 'Winter on the Marsh, Meadow and Mudflat' 1888
Gold-toned gelatin-chloride printing-out-paper
175 × 232 mm The Kodak Museum

This plate is from a series exhibited by Davison in 1888 at the Crystal Palace Exhibition and at the Liverpool Amateur Photographic Association Exhibition. He was awarded a silver medal at both shows. Although photographed on the new, faster gelatin dry plate (which replaced the collodion negative), the exposure time under winter conditions would still have been long – perhaps several seconds – in order to achieve such precision of detail. Davison held the attention of the cows – perhaps with a loud shout – so that they stood stock still (except for their tails). The gelatin-based print shows the characteristic purplish brown colour of gold-toning, and the clean highlights contrast with the yellowed whites of the earlier albumen prints – a defect which would greatly have weakened the wintry atmosphere rendered in the photograph.

George Davison was one of the most influential pictorial photographers practising in the 1890s and 1900s in England, not only through his photographs, which were exhibited at the Photographic Society and later at the Salon (the annual show of The Linked Ring), but also through his writings in the English, American and French photographic journals. He began to take a serious interest in the medium in the mid-1880s. He soon became a successful exhibitor and was also well-known as Secretary of the newly-formed Camera Club (1885). He became a disciple of P.H. Emerson (PLATE 35), adopting the 'Naturalistic' style in which, by use of selective focus, background and foreground detail was subordinated to the main subject.

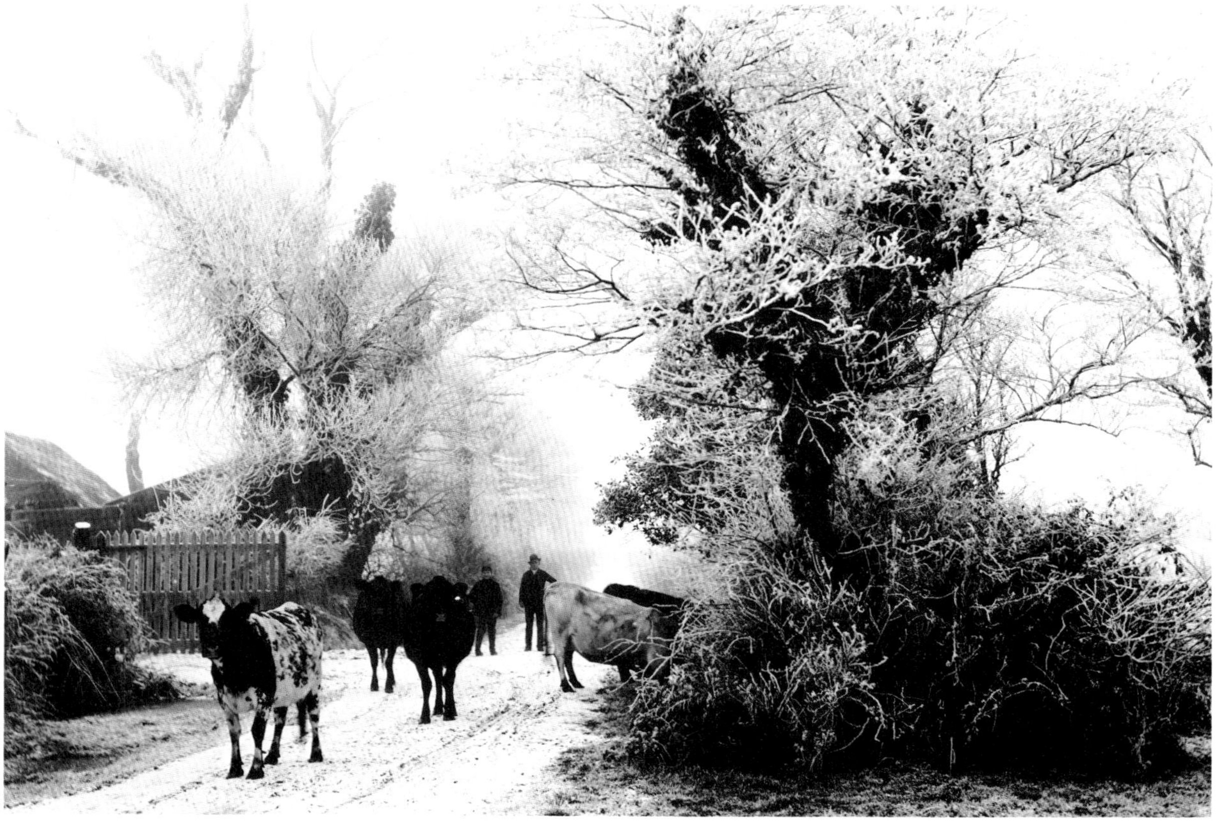

PLATE

18

Paul Martin British 1864–1942
An album of Hampstead scenes 1898
Printing-out paper, gold-toned
Image size 86 × 84 mm Mus. nos. 1839/40–1980 Purchase

These prints are on Solio printing-out paper, the brand supplied by the Eastman Photographic Materials Company in London. They were made from roll film negatives exposed in the NO 2 Falcon camera. They were made in the summer of 1898 at the request of George Davison, then assistant manager of the Eastman company in London, who wished Paul Martin to try out new models of the Kodak roll film cameras. Martin used the NO 2 Falcon box camera and the NO 5 Cartridge Kodak folding camera to photograph street scenes and August Bank Holiday on Hampstead Heath. He found the cameras less easily concealed than his favourite 'Facile' Hand Camera and soon went back to it. The fastest shutter speed of the 'Facile' was 1/20th of a second.

Paul Martin is a representative figure in two ways. He trained as a wood-engraver in the London firm of Paul Douet from 1880–86, when the half-tone process was already beginning to emerge as the new method of mass illustration. In London wood-engraving firms between 1884 and 1899 dropped from 162 to 80 while process-engraving firms grew from 6 to 56. Magazines became a significant market for photographers. Martin established his own photographic illustration firm with H.G. Dorrett in 1899. Looking back in 1939 he recalled: 'Few wood-engravers realised what photography was going to bring in its train. I knew that monster when he was only a sprat, for I took up photography as an amateur in 1884. . . . When the monster made a lunge at me I dodged him and clung to his tail and am still hanging on'. Martin is also an early master of the snapshot, especially of the 'candid' – or covert – variety. 'Instantaneous' photography was a major project of the 1850s. The effort to record life 'on the wing' led to the first application of the shooting term snap-shot to photography by Sir John Herschel in 1860:

> What I have to propose may appear a dream; but it has at least the merit of being a . . . realisable one . . . . It is the . . . representation of scenes in action – the vivid and lifelike reproduction and handing down to the latest posterity of any transaction in real life . . . . I take for granted nothing more than . . . what photography has already realised, or . . . will realise within some very limited lapse of time . . . the possibility of taking a photograph, as it were, by a snap-shot – of securing a picture in a tenth of a second of time.

This projection was fulfilled by Paul Martin and others one generation later.

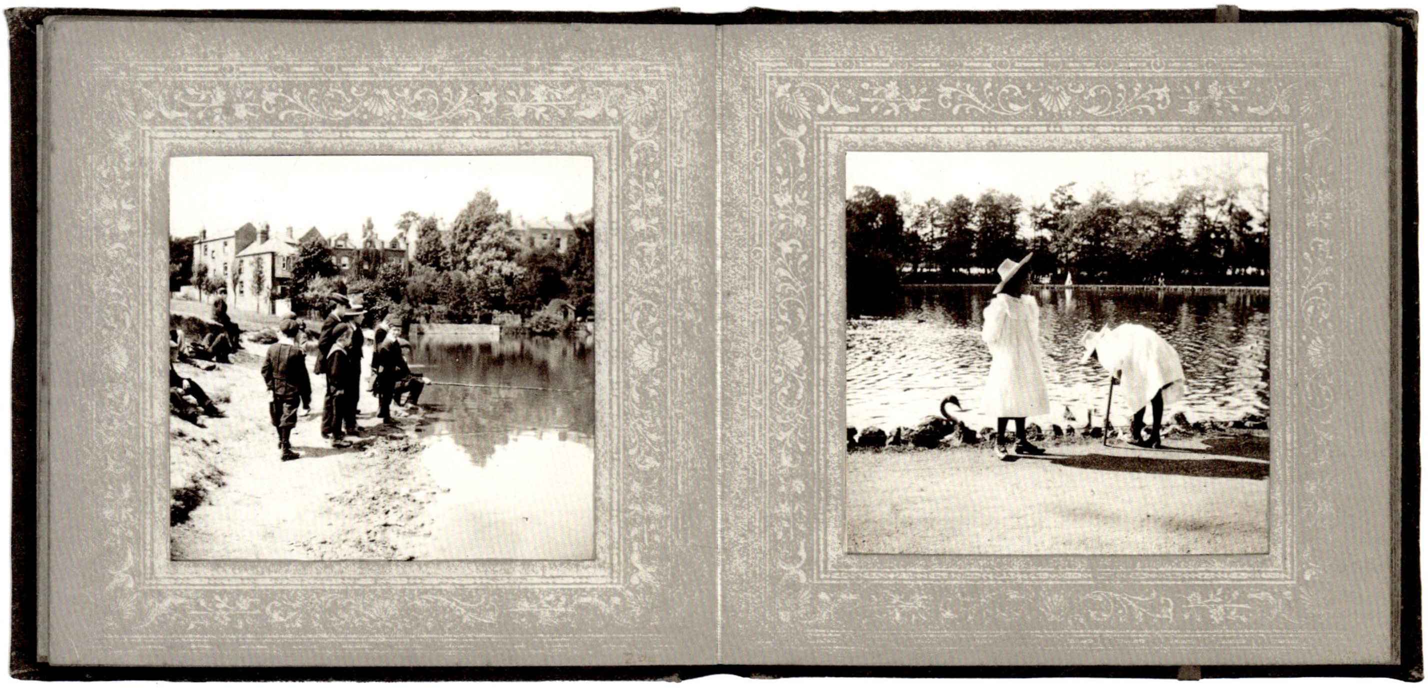

PLATE

19

Frank Meadow Sutcliffe British 1853–1941
Four snapshots of Whitby:
In the harbour, 74 × 96 mm Barrels 74 × 113 mm
The passage 118 × 92.5 mm Quayside fish stall 79 × 136 mm
Solio printing-out paper, gold-toned
The Kodak Museum

Frank Sutcliffe, like Paul Martin (PLATE 18), was asked by George Davison to try out new models of Kodak cameras; unlike Martin, Sutcliffe took to them readily, and between 1898 and 1907 used most models then on the market. He used the very portable held-in-the-hand cameras for his favourite subjects in and around Whitby. He was able to exploit the short exposure times – for example to catch reflections in the water, which would have been lost in a time exposure. The hand-held camera could be used from a height or viewpoint which would not have been easy with the tripod-bound plate camera. Sutcliffe's snapshots were printed on Solio printing-out paper, with gold toning. They show some of the variations in image colour to be found in printing-out paper prints.

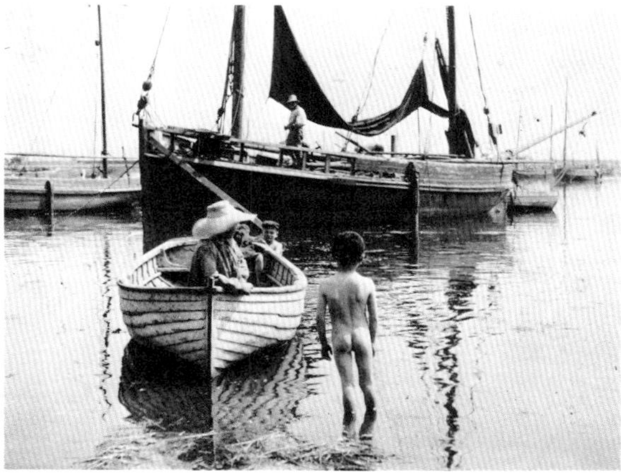
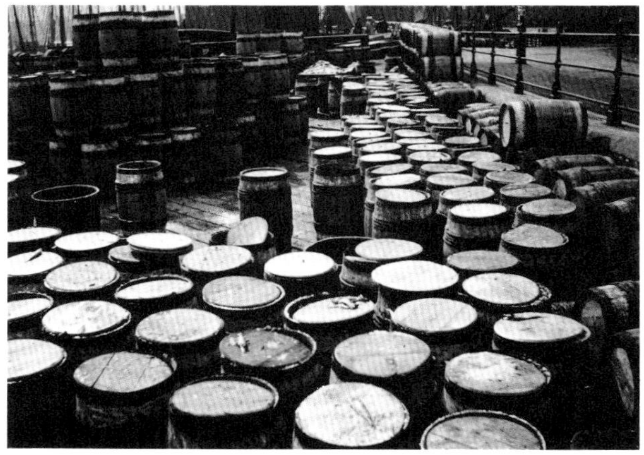
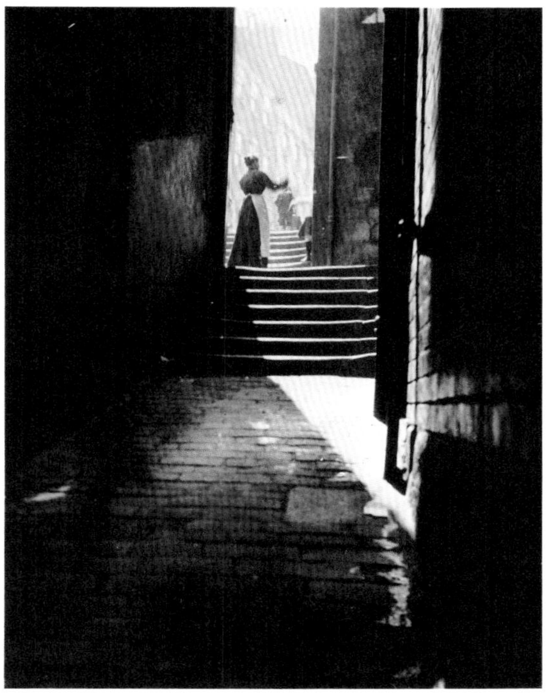
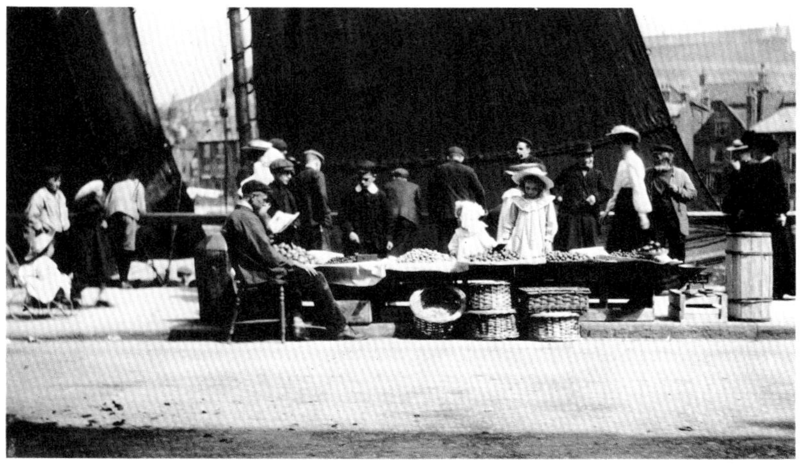

PLATE

20

Edward Steichen American 1879–1973
Mother and Child – Sunlight 1905
Printing-out paper and gelatin silver bromide prints
88 × 111 mm and 86.5 × 111 mm (reproduced same size) The Kodak Museum

This photograph took first prize in a Kodak competition in 1905. All entries were required to have been produced with Kodak materials (camera, negative, printing paper). Steichen used the new 'non-curl' roll film and contact printed the negative in two ways. One is on Solio printing-out paper and shows the characteristic purplish-brown colour of the gold-toned, printed-out image. The other was printed on gelatin-silver bromide paper and developed, giving a black and white image. Gelatin-based printing-out and development papers came into general use in the 1880s. Although printing-out papers continued in use at least until the Second World War there was a general transition throughout the 1920s and 1930s to the use of development papers. These did not require strong daylight for printing and, in the case of gelatin-silver bromide papers, permitted enlargements from small negatives.

Steichen's *contre-jour* snapshot of his wife and daughter was one of 28,000 entries to the Kodak competition and received a prize of £30. (*Kodaking* by Alfred Stieglitz came third). The photograph was published in photogravure in *Camera Work* in April 1906; Steichen also printed it in platinum. The photograph, both intimate and elevated in sentiment, is characteristic of much of the art photography of the Photo-Secession and of the milder forms of late Impressionism to which it is closely related. Such sweet moments of family life in *la belle époque*, at once idyllic and instantaneous, recur in the pages of *Camera Work* not merely to lighten its more weighty themes – but as a persistent value.

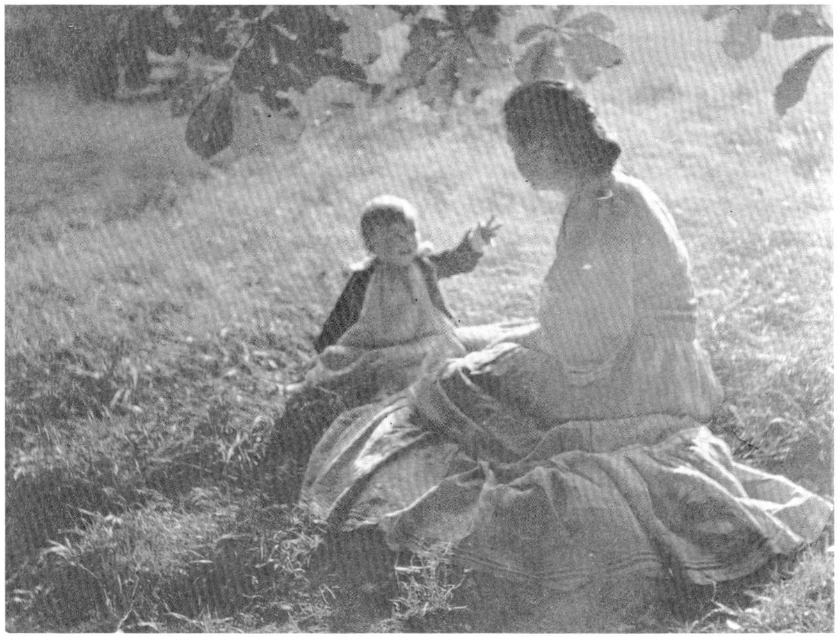

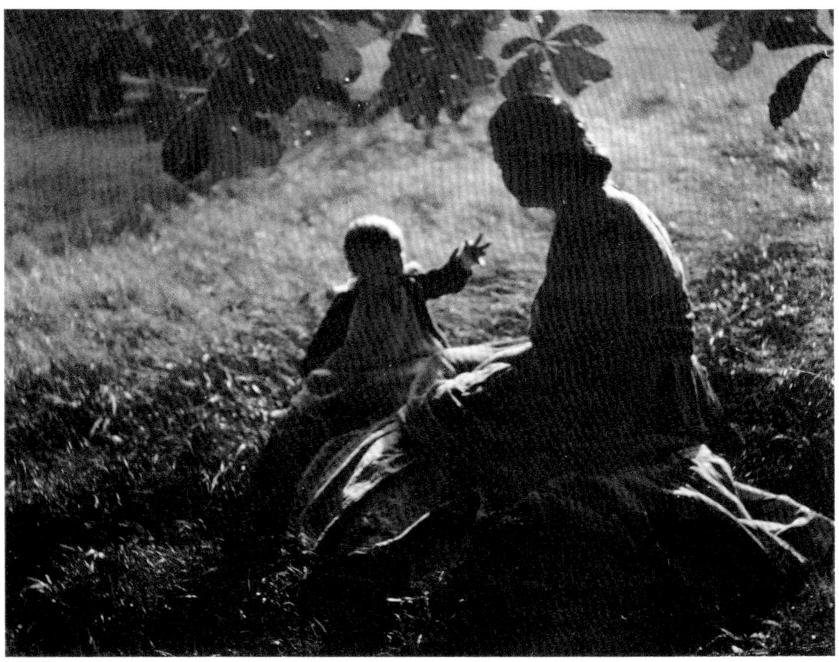

PLATE

21

Lewis Hine American 1874–1940
Immigrant family, New York City Probably 1905–10
Gelatin silver bromide
176 × 126 mm (reproduced same size) The Kodak Museum

Lewis Hine regularly supplied his documentary photographs as straight contact prints from half-plate ($4\frac{3}{4} \times 6\frac{1}{2}$ inches; 121 × 166mm) glass plate negatives. Normally, to be suitable for reproduction, they were on glossy paper. This photograph of a cheerful immigrant family was masked to an oval and printed on a cream-based gelatin-silver bromide paper. The black and white developed image has been toned to a sepia colour. The toning process most commonly used employed sodium sulphide solution, which produces hydrogen sulphide – the gas with the 'rotten eggs' smell. Toning large numbers of prints called for stamina on the part of the operator.

Lewis Hine began his project of photographing immigrants to the United States in 1904, often photographing at Ellis Island with magnesium flash powder. He first began to use a camera as an educational tool as teacher of nature studies and geography at the Ethical Culture School in New York. The mass immigration from Central and Eastern Europe which flowed through the narrow conduit of Ellis Island was a phenomenon in itself but Hine's project to photograph there was a response to the desire of the principal of his school to instil in pupils a regard for contemporary immigrants comparable with that automatically conferred on the Pilgrims who landed at Plymouth Rock. His photographs individualised, to some extent at least, constituents of the mass migration from the bogs and *shtetls* of Europe; in this case printing technique bestows a benevolent aura on his subject.

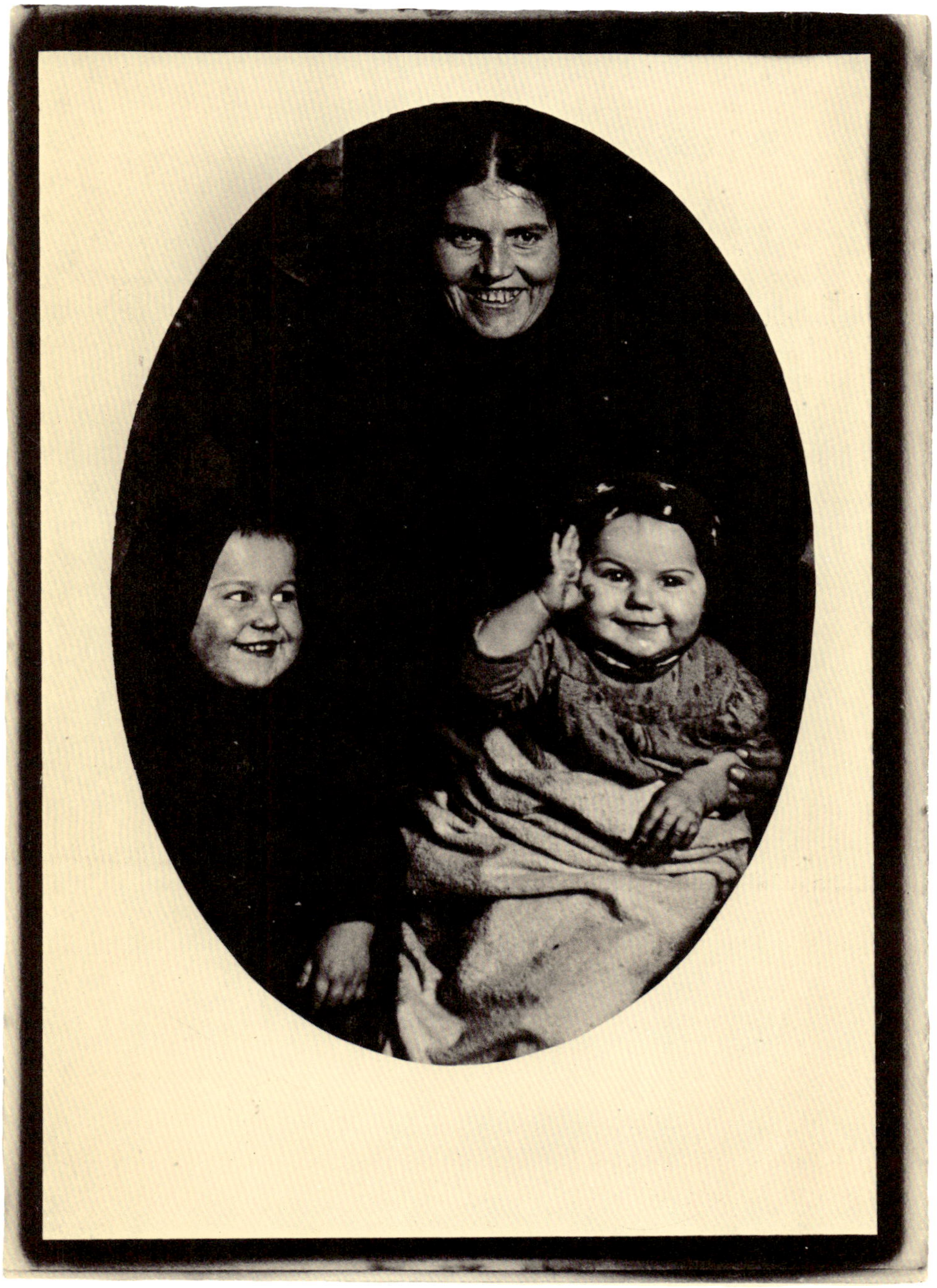

PLATE

22

Andrew Pitcairn-Knowles British 1871–1956
The Brussels Dog Market About 1900
Rabbit Racing (?) Belgium (?) About 1910
Toned Gelatin silver chloride or 'Gaslight' paper prints
Both 119 × 164 mm (reproduced same size) Mus. nos. Ph 313/314–1982
Given by Mr and Mrs Richard Pitcairn-Knowles

Contact printing gelatin papers usually employed silver chloride. Often called 'Gaslight' papers, they could be handled in subdued artificial light, and required only a short exposure to a gaslamp or electric light, followed by development to give a cold-toned black and white image. Most contact printing papers had glossy or at least smooth surfaces to ensure proper contact between the negative and the paper in the printing frame. Textured papers were used for enlarging, where the negative was projected onto the paper; since greater sensitivity was needed, enlarging papers were, and still are, made using silver bromide. These examples were contact printed on glossy gelatin silver chloride paper, toned to change the image colour from the rather cold neutral tones characteristic of the paper.

Andrew Pitcairn-Knowles was born in Rotterdam, educated in England and Germany, and lived with his wife and son in Berlin, Brussels and Paris. He wrote articles for *Wide World Magazine, Outing, Badminton Magazine, Illustrated Sporting and Dramatic News,* and himself launched *Sport im Bild* in Berlin in 1895. He took photographs to illustrate his articles, which covered such topics as sand yachting in Belgium, the animal markets in Paris and Brussels, badger baiting in Germany, cider-making, motor racing and the Derby. The second photograph here appears to present a race in which rabbits on leading ribbons are urged forward with special cues by patient rival owners. Pitcairn-Knowles occupies a position at the beginning of the era of photo-journalism, providing picture stories for specialist magazines and for the popular 'human interest' illustrated press of the early half-tone period. His activities in photography came to an end with the outbreak of the First World War, when he established a 'Hydro' at Hastings.

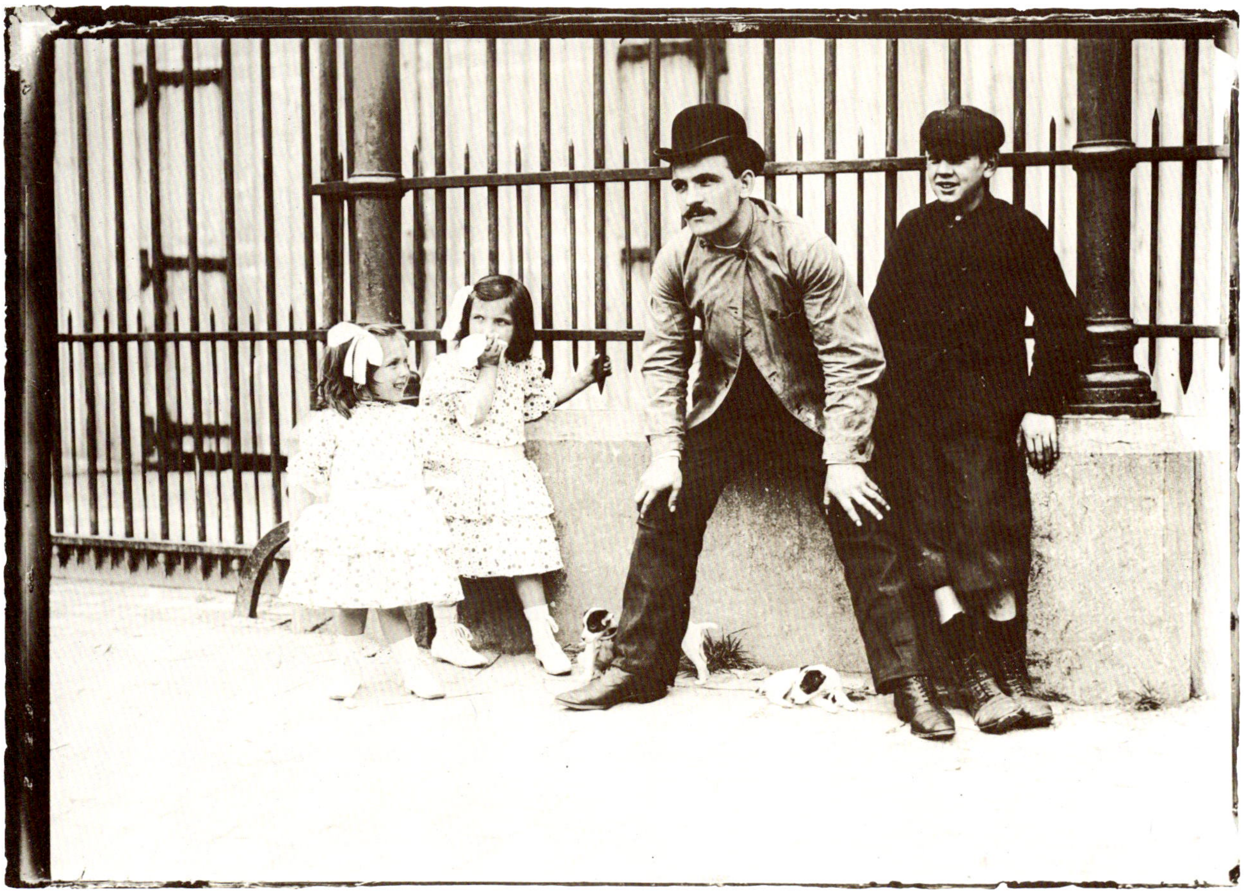

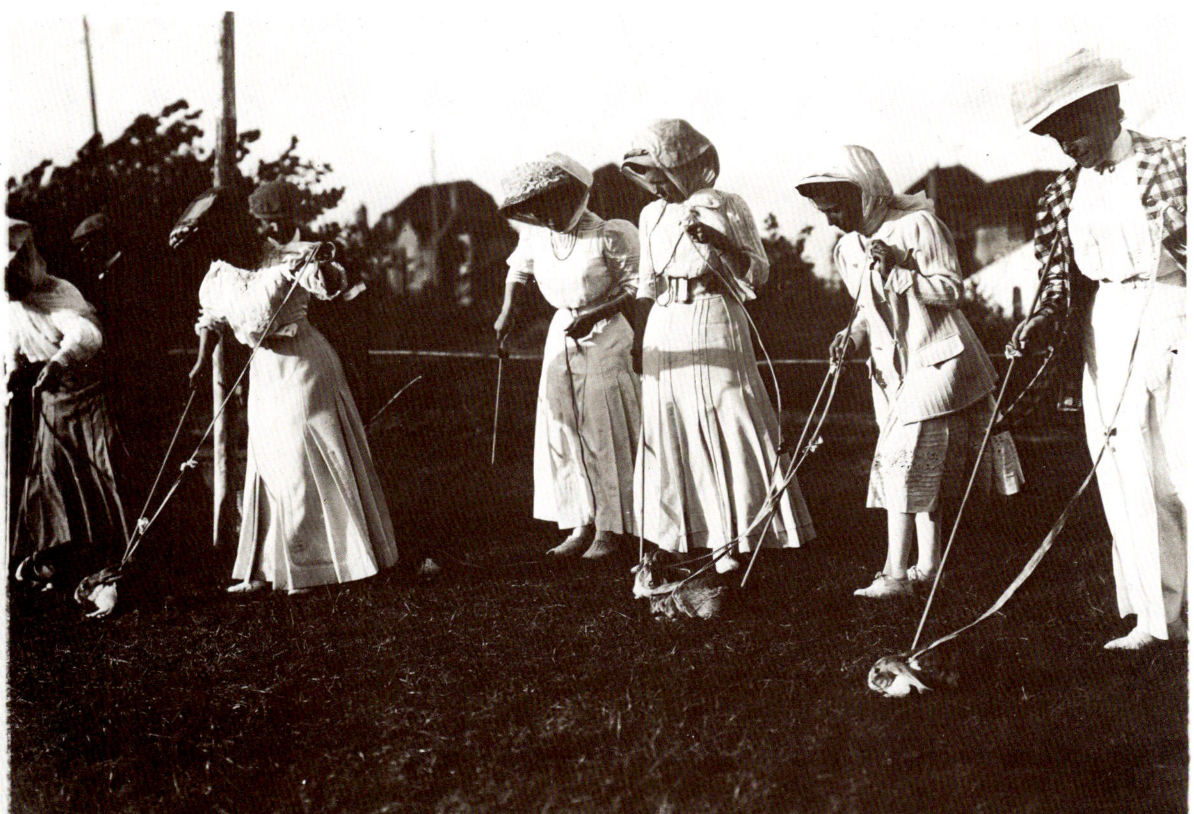

PLATE
23

Lewis Hine American 1874–1940
The Cop and the Gang 1920s (?)
Gelatin silver print
196 × 251 mm The Kodak Museum

Although Lewis Hine supplied most of his photographs as contact prints (PLATE 21) for use as magazine illustrations he did make some enlargements. This street scene was enlarged on a medium-glossy gelatin-silver paper. The warm tones of the earlier photographic processes, inherent in the printing-out processes, began to be replaced by black and white images. These are comparable only with the developed salt prints of the 1850s such as PLATE 6. Public acceptance of the black and white photographic print was no doubt helped by the increasing use of photography in newspapers and magazines from the early years of the century.

The print is stamped on reverse 'Lewis Wickes Hine – Interpretive Photography'. By 1907 Hine was simultaneously studying sociology at Columbia University and working on his first assignment for The National Child Labor Committee. Exploitation in sweatshops was an almost inevitable sequel to arrival at Ellis Island. His photography for the NCLC was used for its own publications, periodical magazines and newspapers, slides for lectures and for exhibition display boards with text. He adopted his 'Interpretive Photography' stamp in 1919–20 which reflected an interest in a photography no longer strictly documentary in intent. Hine is not concerned here with enforcing child labour laws but in making a photograph which combines group portraiture, environmental interaction and a still from an imaginary film.

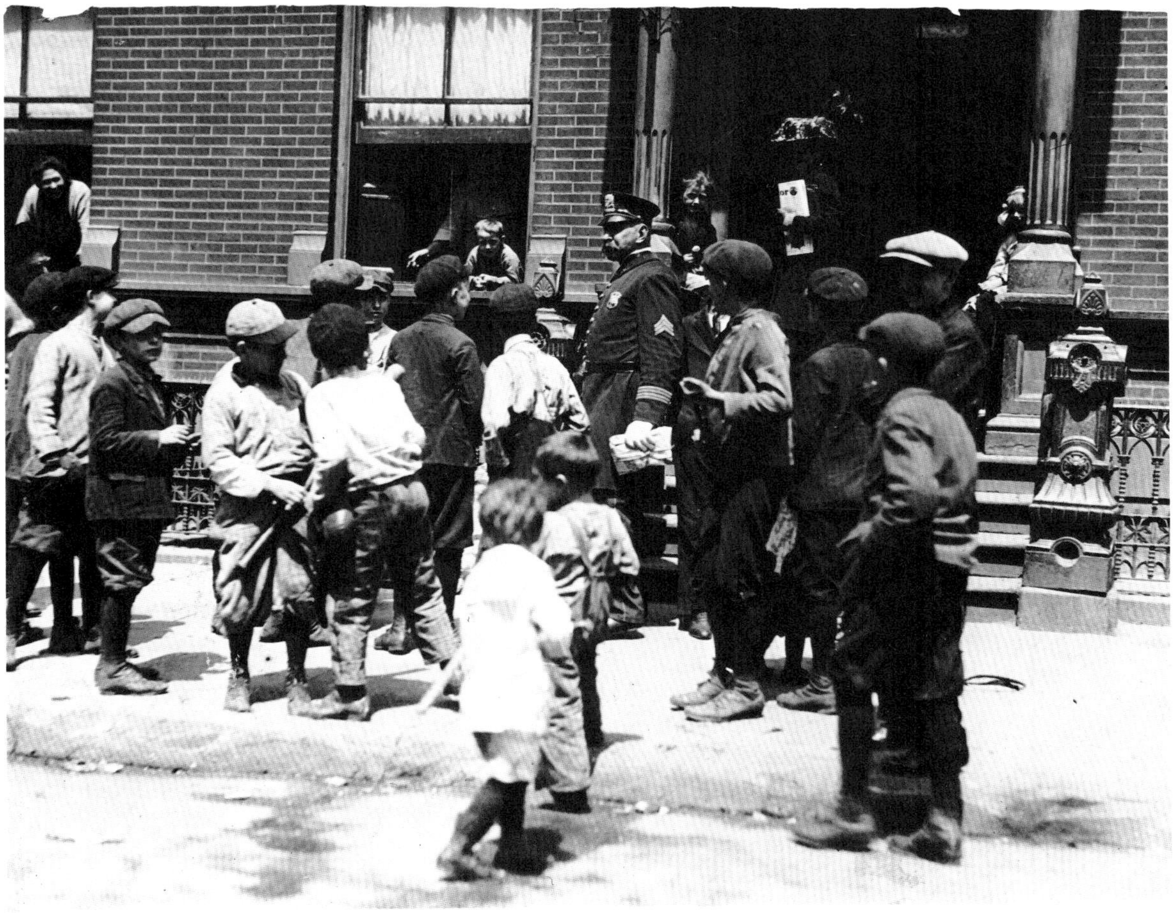

PLATE

24

Anna Atkins British 1797–1871
'Festuca ovina' (fescue grass; sheep's grass) 1854
Cyanotype (blueprint)
351 × 248 mm Mus. no. 380–1981 Purchase

The cyanotype, or blueprint, process was invented by the astronomer and scientist Sir John Herschel, whose many contributions to the early development of photography included the discovery in 1819 that sodium thiosulphate (or hyposulphite as it was then known) was a solvent for silver salts – a fact which later was to make possible the 'fixing' of photographs to make them permanent – and to this day thiosulphates are still used for this purpose. In 1842 Sir John found that paper impregnated with iron salts was light sensitive, prussian blue being formed in the paper. At the time, the cyanotype process was little used, except for printing 'photograms', like this example. From the 1880s it was used for copying engineering and architectural drawings, for which it was well suited, since it gave best results from an original of high contrast. In this application, the process continued into recent times, when it was superseded by diazo, and more recently, electrostatic copying. For some years, especially in the 1890s and 1900s, it was used by amateurs for proofing snapshot negatives, but the low contrast of the process often gave rather muddied results, and the strong blue colour was not suitable for many subjects.

Anna Atkins was the daughter of the zoologist John George Children F.R.S., who was present at both of the meetings of the Royal Society at which Fox Talbot outlined his new process of 'photogenic drawing' in February 1839. The family received calotype specimens from Talbot in 1841 and was associated also with Sir John Herschel. The major practitioner to make use of cyanotype in the early period was Anna Atkins. She was a skilled scientific draughtsman (contributing the drawings of shells for her father's translation of Lamarck's *Genera of Shells* 1823) and botanist. Cyanotype proved to be the ideal method of recording specimens from her extensive herbarium. Her best-known work, *British Algae: Cyanotype Impressions* was privately issued in instalments beginning in October 1843 and its author wrote in the introduction: 'the difficulty of making accurate drawings of objects as minute as many of the Algae and Conferva, has induced me to avail myself of Sir John Herschel's beautiful process of Cyanotype, to obtain impressions of the plants themselves, which I have much pleasure in offering to my botanical friends'. The series was completed in 1854. The present plate is from an album of British and Foreign Flowering Plants and Ferns presented by Anna Atkins to 'A.D.', a member of the family of the pioneer photographer Henry Dixon, in 1854. The specimen was laid on the sensitised sheet and exposed to sunlight for a few minutes. This produced a faint image which was brought out to a rich blue and made permanent simply by washing the paper in plain water.

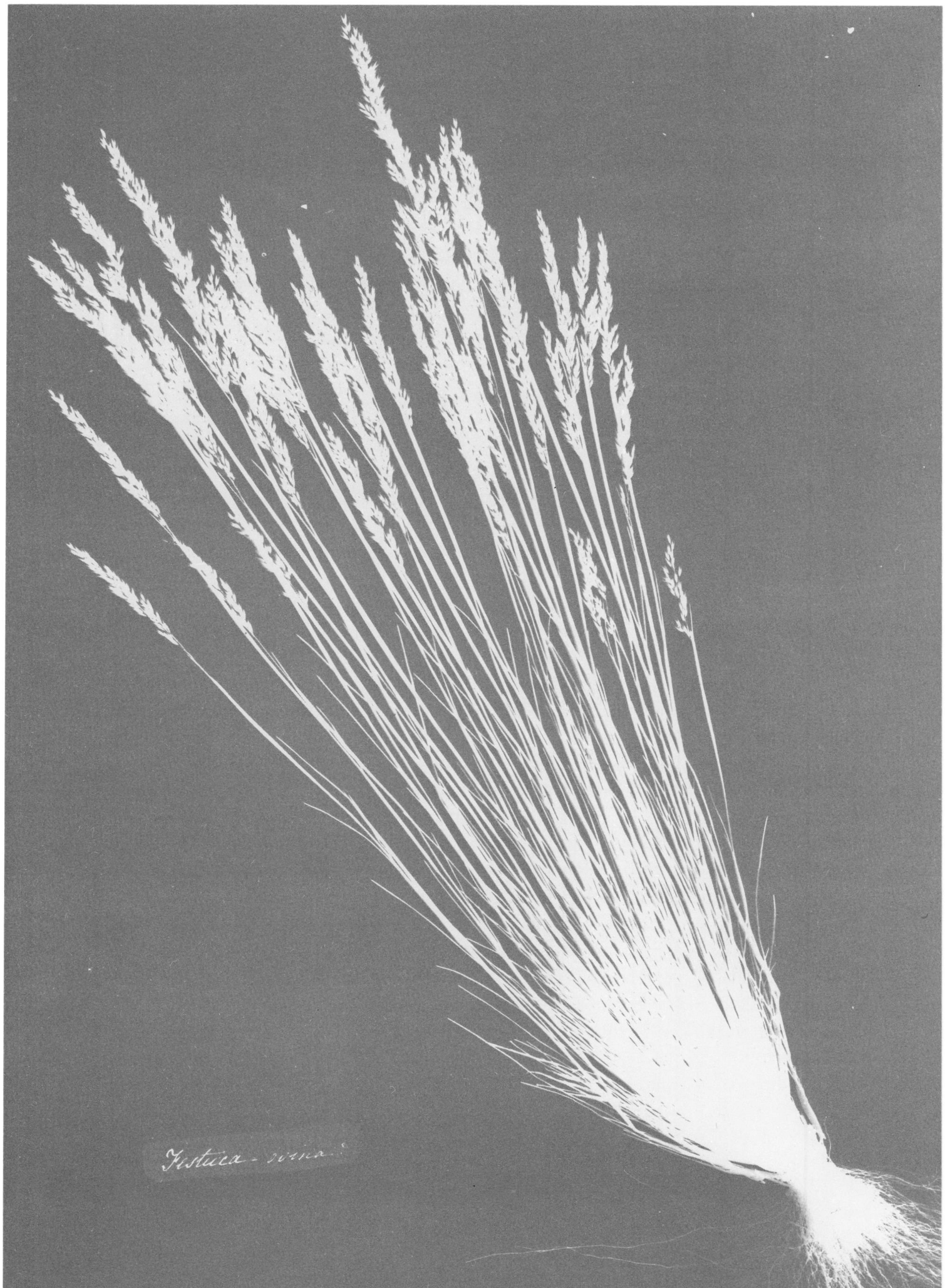
Festuca ovina

PLATE

25

Frederick Hollyer British 1837–1933
Two portraits of John Ruskin 1894
Platinum prints
165 × 124 mm and 155 × 123 mm Mus. nos. 7602/3–1938
Given by Miss E. M. Hollyer

The platinum process invented by William Willis in 1873 was used to make prints of particularly fine quality. As in the salted paper process, platinum prints were made on paper impregnated, rather than coated, with light-sensitive chemicals – in this case compounds of iron rather than silver. A form of development after exposure produced finely divided platinum in the paper. The intense black colour of platinum formed in this way gave the shadows a very rich tone, while the lighter greys had an almost silvery tone. However, if the development process was carried out at high temperature the form of the platinum deposited in the paper was changed and the image colour became warmer. The hot-process prints ranged in colour from a warm neutral to a pronounced sepia. These two portraits show the conventional and 'hot-process' forms. In the 1890s platinum printing was the most popular process for exhibition prints at the Royal Photographic Society annual exhibition. Between 1893 and 1899 almost half of the exhibited prints were on platinum paper. The paper became prohibitively expensive when the cost of platinum rose drastically during the First World War.

Frederick Hollyer was a master craftsman in the field of copying paintings and drawings, taking the major medal in this class at the Exposition Universelle in 1889. His most extensive series illustrated the oeuvres of Burne-Jones, Watts and Rossetti. He also photographed the artists and their families. His portraiture offers a platinum-period parallel to the earlier achievement of Carjat (PLATE 30), providing a pantheon of English painters, intellectuals, actresses and fellow photographers in the last quarter of the 19th century. In 1920 he assembled three chintz-covered albums of his portraits for his daughter Eleanour. The first album opens with these portraits of Ruskin – the warm-toned print representing Ruskin as a genial grandee, the cooler print showing the reclusive culture-hero whose writings dominated the period of Pre-Raphaelitism and the Arts and Crafts Movement. The third album is concluded by a self-portrait taken in 1920. The cooler Ruskin portrait here is cropped from the squarer original which Hollyer sold in two sizes and in both platinum and carbon. He also printed in the Twenties on bromide paper but pointed out that it did not have 'the fine mezzotint quality' of platinum.

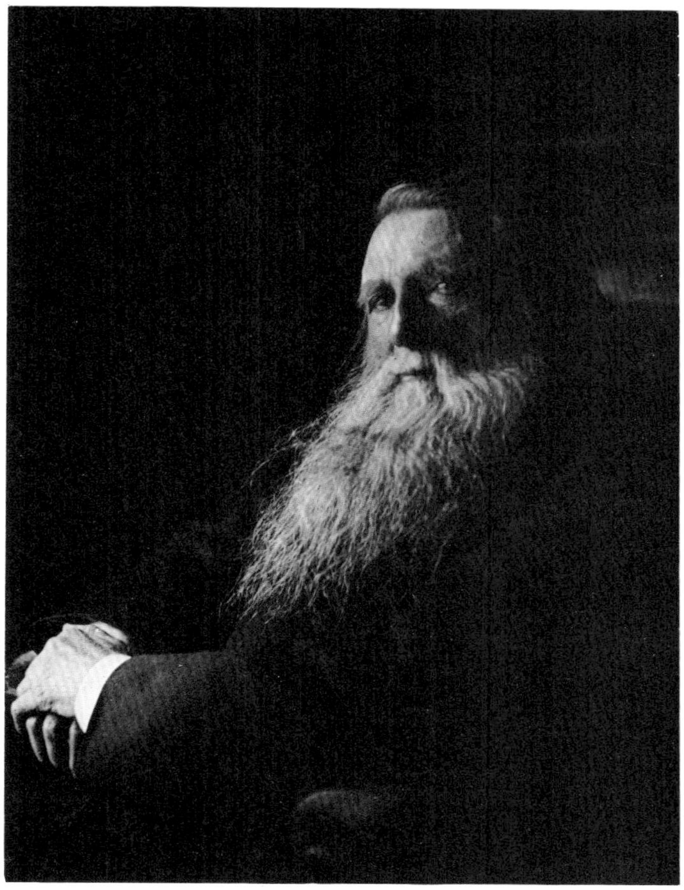
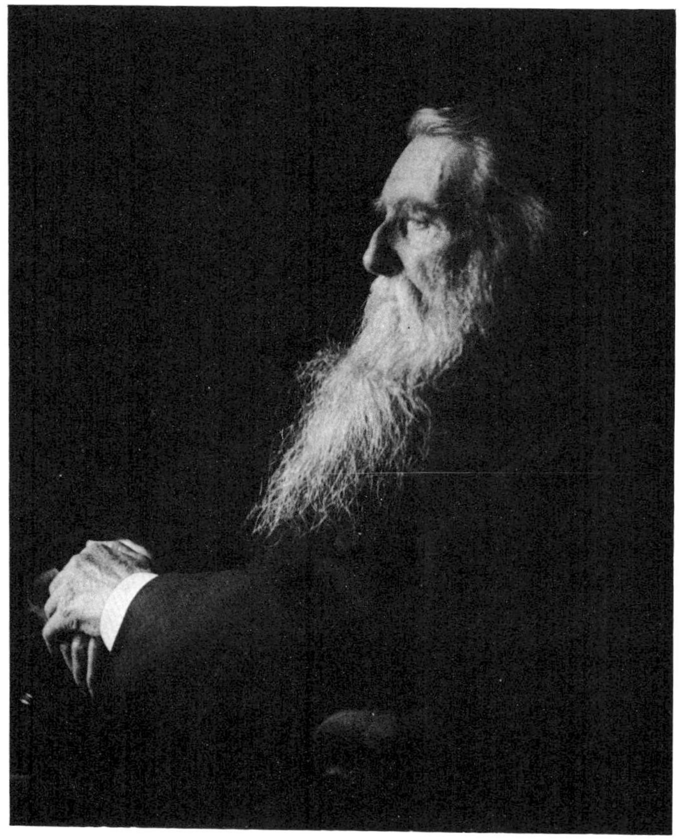

PLATE

26

Paul Martin British 1864–1944
Rough weather at Hastings 1896
Platinum print from an album
68 × 94 mm (reproduced same size) Mus. no.x.549 Purchase

Platinum paper was used for the contact printing even of small snapshot negatives. For example, George Bernard Shaw had a high proportion of his developed roll films printed as a matter of course on platinum paper. This example shows the characteristic clean white highlights and wide tonal range of the platinum print. It shows no sign of image deterioration despite the damaged state of the album from which it comes. The album suffered from damp storage resulting in foxing of the pages and considerable fading of printing-out paper prints but the platinum prints remain pristine.

Paul Martin used the 'Facile' hand-camera to photograph waves – exceptionally large ones – at Hastings. He showed these in lantern slide form at camera club meetings in the 1890s. Forty years later a reviewer recalled that 'Perhaps of all the slides shown, the most arresting were several depicting terrific seas breaking over the esplanades, for nothing better in their way has, probably, ever been done'. 'Rough weather' became a favourite postcard genre. Martin's camera survived by virtue of its leather case and an ebonite lens cover he had added and he himself by virtue of the change of clothes he kept drying in the kitchen of his hotel. This is a milder example than some in the series but it suggests the excellent qualities of platinum in rendering the silvery tones of agitated seas.

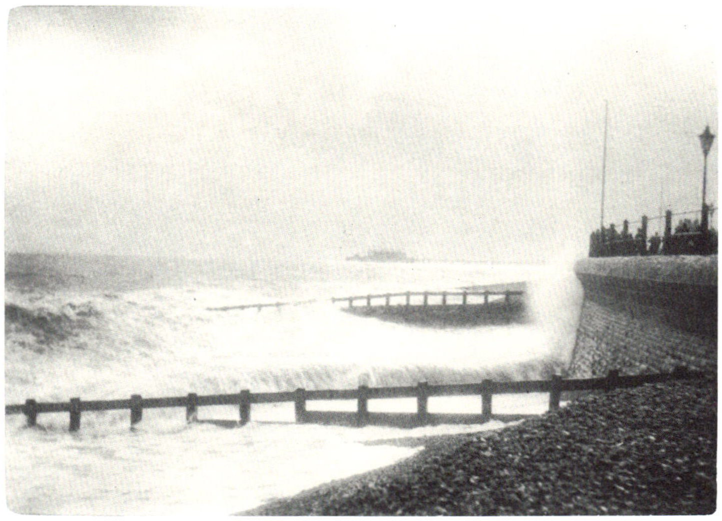

PLATE

27

Camille Silvy French, born 1835 (active 1858–68)
Proclamation of the Army for Italy 1859
Phototype (Joubert's process)
Image size 139 × 112 mm (reproduced same size) Mus. no. Ph. 230–1982 Purchase
Mount Lettered: 'Phototype Process / Photographed from Nature by C. Silvy / This print in Permanent Ink / is presented by Mr F. Joubert / to the Subscribers of the Photographic Journal / London 15th January 1860'

This print did not, in the event, appear until June 1860. The reason appears to have been that a certain amount of light was required to make the prints by Joubert's process and a total of 3,000 was required. Joubert was a French engraver working in London. Like many other inventors at this period he sought a method of accurate and rapid photographic reproduction. He also patented a method of making glass pictures which made the production of photographic stained glass windows seem to be a possibility. His Phototype process was much admired but no one came forward to reward the inventor, as he had reasonable hopes would occur, and the process remained – and remains – secret. It appears to have much in common with the collotype (see GLOSSARY). A relatively rapid photo-mechanical process like Phototype could have been used in the publication of topical photographs. Joubert chose to reproduce a photograph by his associate Camille Silvy – who was strongly interested in multiple-production – which has all the characteristics of a news photograph. Parisian workmen are shown – apparently posed by Silvy – looking at a proclamation about the sending of the French Imperial army to Italy in the interest of the Northern Italian states against Austria. Louis Napoleon's invasion received liberal and radical approval and conservative opposition and could be regarded as a turning point in the internal politics of the Second Empire.

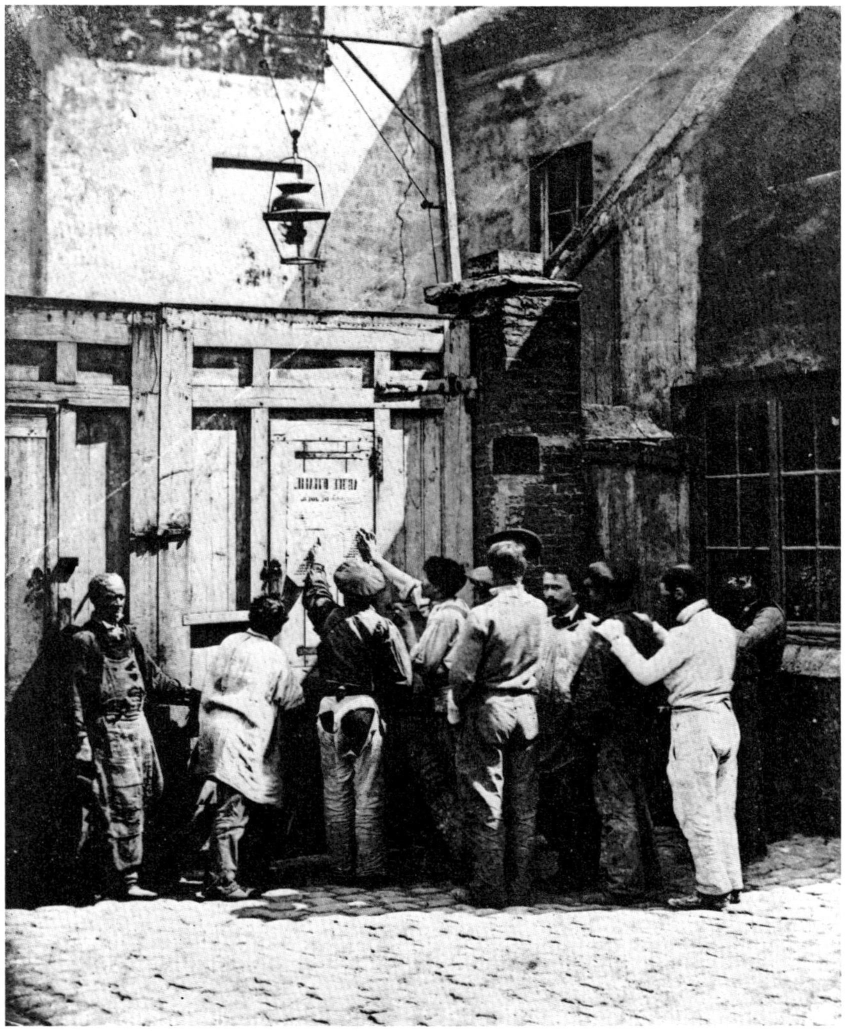

PLATE

28

John Thomson British 1837–1921
London Nomades 1876
Woodburytype
109 × 83 mm (reproduced same size) Mus. no. Ph. 315–1982 Given by Mrs Dorothy Crisp

Walter Woodbury's Woodburytype process was a variation on the carbon process in which a relief image in gelatin was pressed into a lead block to form a mould. Gelatinous ink applied to the mould could be transferred to paper to give a continuous tone, permanent image. The usual image colour was a chocolate brown, but as with the carbon process, almost any colour pigment could be used. This example is typical. Woodburytype images often show clear signs of the relief image, especially at the edges between dark and light areas. They were always mounted on book or journal pages, or on card mounts, usually with a process credit beneath the print or at least on the title page or elsewhere in the book. Unlike the carbon process, the Woodburytype was not used by amateurs, because of the need for presses to form and print from the lead moulds.

This picture inaugurated one of the most famous photographic part-works of the 19th century, *Street Life in London*. The series began in February 1877 and 36 monthly instalments appeared. Each contained one photograph, printed by the Woodburytype method, plus a three page essay written by Adolphe Smith, a journalist, or by Thomson himself. Mayhew's *London Labour and the London Poor* (1851) was illustrated by woodcuts, some based on Daguerreotypes. Thomson noted that 'The precision and accuracy of photography enables us to present true types of the London poor and shield us from the accusation of either underrating or exaggerating individual peculiarities of appearance'.

Thomson wrote of the 'Nomades' that they were allied to but distinct from true gipsies. The photograph was taken on waste ground in Battersea and represents 'a friendly group gathered round the caravan of William Hampton, a man who enjoys the reputation among his fellows of being "a fair-spoken, honest gentleman".' A few weeks later Thomson returned to Battersea with his photograph of the group which he presented to Hampton: '"Bless ye! he exclaimed, that's old Mary Pradd, sitting on the steps of the wan [sic], wot was murdered in the Borough, middle of last month"'. The precise manner of her apparently violent death was not established. Thomson noted that, 'Clean and respectable in her dress, she might in her youth have been even of comely appearance, but now she wore the indelible stamp of a woman who had been dulled and deadened by a hard life' (and had taken to drink). *Street Life in London* stands at the beginning of photo-journalism and, perhaps inevitably, begins with a sensational death.

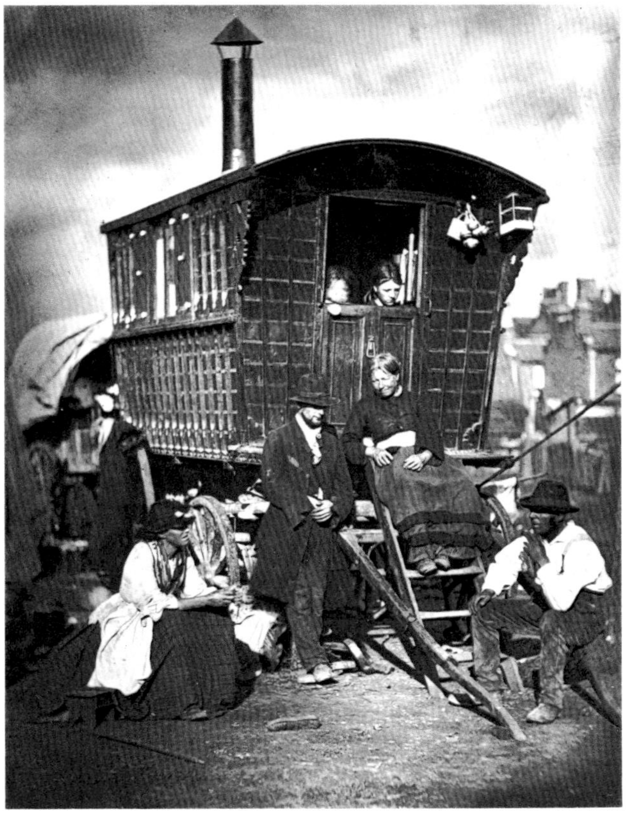

PLATE

29

Léon Vidal French 1834–1906
Portrait of a lady 1879
Photochrome
129 × 89 mm (reproduced same size) The Kodak Museum

Léon Vidal developed the Photochrome printing process in the 1870s as a method of accurately colouring photographs for quantity reproduction. From the original negative a number of copy negatives were made, on glass or thin paper. On each negative, those areas which were not to be coloured in a particular hue were blocked out with an opaque medium. For example, on the negative prepared for the colour blue, only those areas to be coloured blue in the final print remained uncovered. Negatives were prepared for as many colours as required – up to twelve. These negatives were used to make lithographic tint plates which were then employed to transfer colours in succession either to a monochromatic printing from an un-retouched negative or, as here, to a photograph (in this case a Woodburytype). This example was made with twelve superimposed colour printings. The most notable series by Vidal is devoted to national treasures from the great museums of France rendered with meticulous attention to colour.

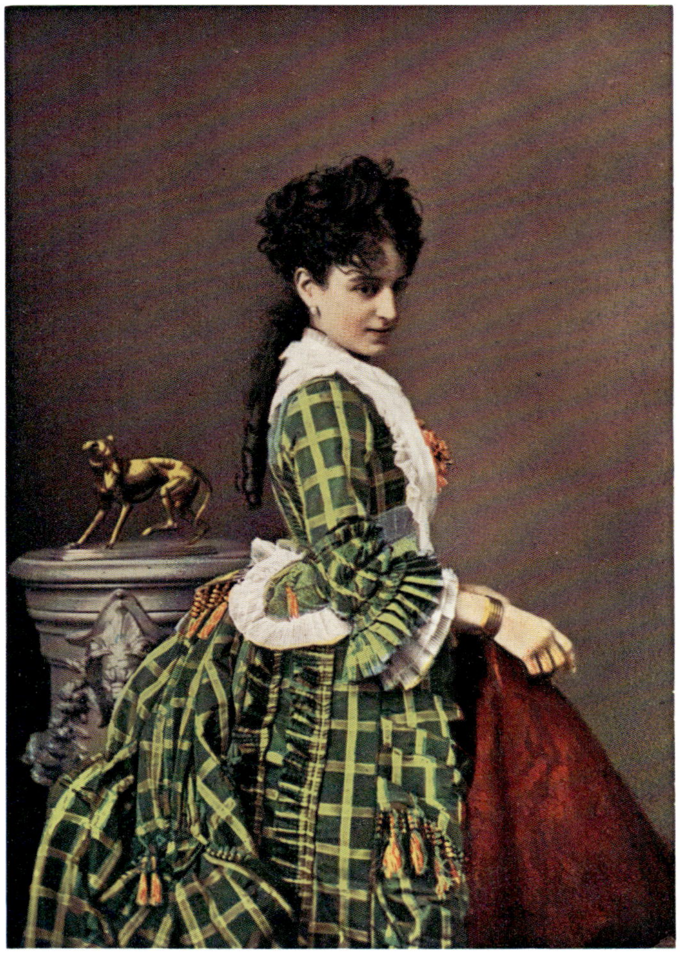

PLATE

30

Étienne Carjat French 1828–1906
Charles Baudelaire (1821–67) About 1862
Carbon print published in 'Galerie Contemporaine' 1878
232 × 183 mm (reproduced same size) Mus. no. 1190–1980 Purchase

The tendency of silver images to deteriorate, especially when imperfectly processed, made the search for a truly permanent photographic process a burning issue in the second half of the last century. Several solutions emerged. One was the platinum print; another was the carbon process, perfected in the 1860s. The carbon print consisted of a permanent pigment (in any one of a very wide range of colours) in a gelatin layer of varying thickness. The process was a little tricky to manipulate but the results were completely permanent. Carbon printing was widely employed for book illustration and commercial editions of prints from the 1860s (notably by Julia Margaret Cameron).

This example is typical, with the most common colour of carbon prints – a chocolate brown.

This portrait of Baudelaire has controlled much of his posthumous representation both by artists and in the minds of his readers. The poet was on good terms with the writer, editor and caricaturist Carjat, whose portrait photography provides an inspired conspectus of the Paris intelligentsia in the 1850s and 1860s. Baudelaire wrote to Carjat: 'It [the portrait] is not perfect, because such perfection is impossible, but I have rarely seen anything as good.' He wrote at some length to his mother on one occasion, urging her to have her portrait taken but 'It is necessary *that I should be present. You don't know about it*, and all the photographers, even the excellent ones, have ridiculous manias; they take for a good image an image in which all the warts, all the wrinkles, all the defects, all the trivialities of the face are rendered very visible . . . . There are hardly any even in Paris who could manage what I want, that is to say a portrait that is exact but having the softness of touch (*flou*) of a drawing. Now, let us think about this shall we?'

Carjat's portrait meets these demands and permanently records its subject's severe mouth, immoderate brow and the eyes a contemporary described as two drops of coffee (*deux gouttes de café*).

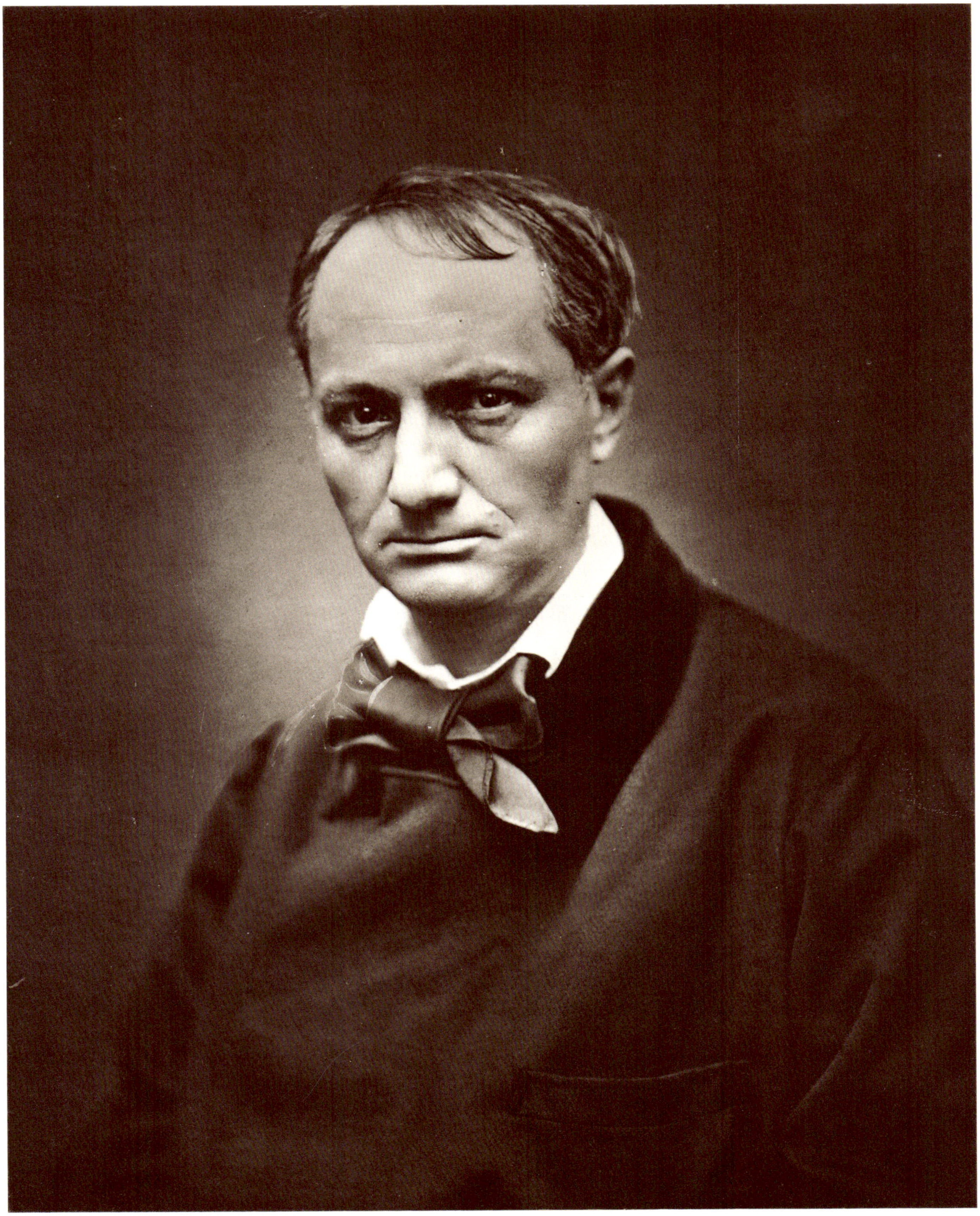

PLATE

31

Heinrich Kühn German, worked Austria 1866–1944
Portrait of Alfred Stieglitz 1907
Oil pigment print
289 × 227 mm Mus. no. 38–1977 Purchase

The variations of the oil pigment process, which relied on the selective taking up off fatty inks or oil-based pigments by a selectively hardened gelatin layer, are difficult to distinguish from each other, at least from their end products, especially since the ink image was often transferred to a paper or tissue sheet. This example is almost certainly by the oil pigment process in which an inked-up gelatin relief was used to transfer the ink image to a thin paper tissue. The oil pigment process used contact printing from a large negative to produce the gelatin relief. The later Bromoil process allowed prints to be made from small negatives by enlargement.

This portrait was made in his studio in Innsbruck by the leader of Austrian art photography, whose prints were collected and published by the leader of American art photography, Alfred Stieglitz. In the summer of 1907 Kühn and the Americans Frank Eugene, Edward Steichen and Stieglitz experimented together with the new Autochrome process in Bavaria. In the same year also Stieglitz's journey to Europe resulted in his famous photograph *The Steerage*, which represented his commitment to straight photography and modern subject matter. He had little stylistic influence on Kühn and it has been suggested that his main importance for Kühn may have been as the exemplar of the photographic impresario. The manipulative oil pigment process allowed Kühn to represent the cloaked figure of Stieglitz as a personage rising out of and above darkness, an aesthete of the Pictorialist epoch. Two years later Kühn achieved a triumph by arranging for the acquisition of photographs from the artistic section of the 1909 International Exhibition by the Dresden Museum, a precedent applauded by Stieglitz in the pages of *Camera Work*.

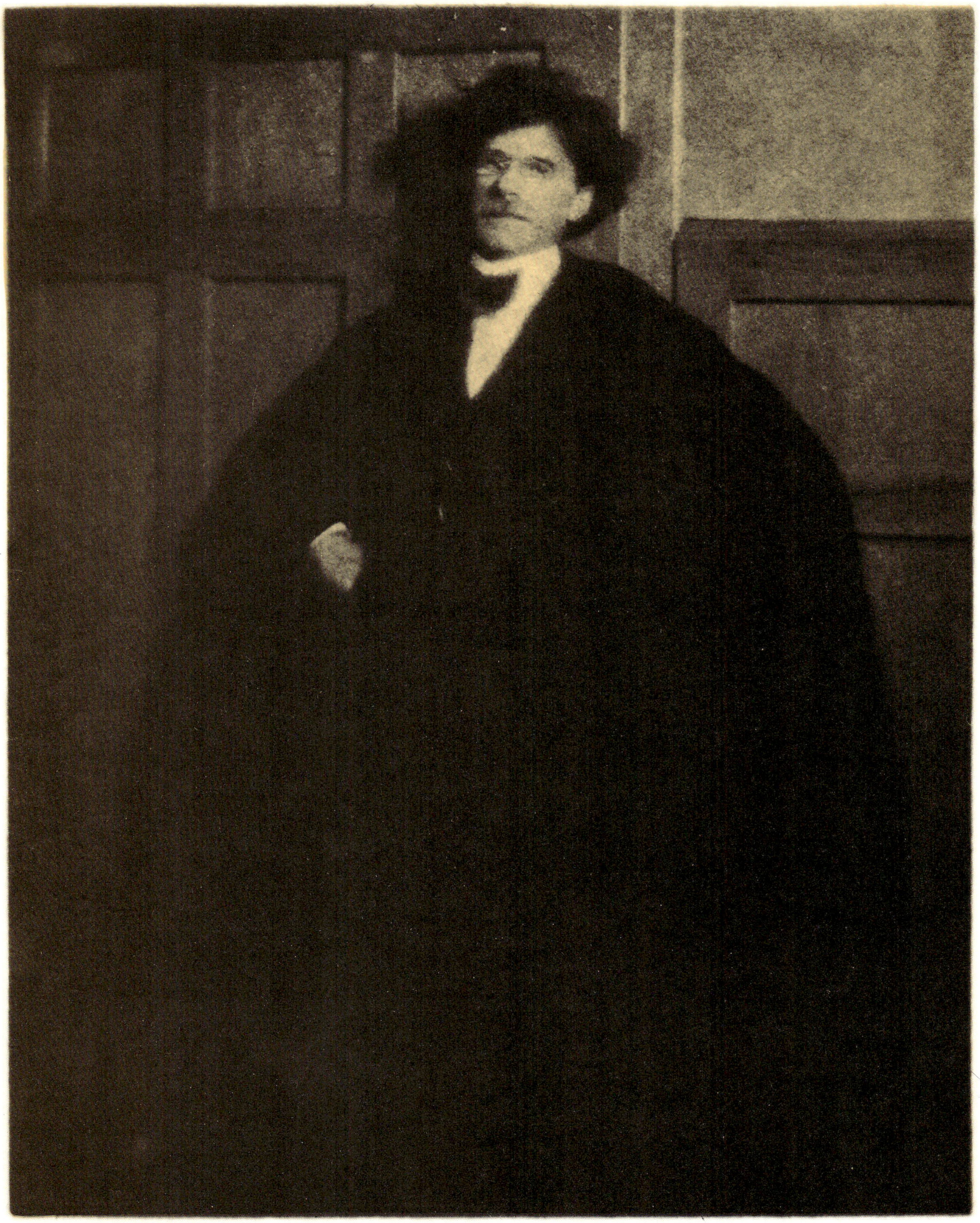

PLATE

32

Robert Demachy French 1859–1936
A Study in Red About 1898
Gum bichromate print
159 × 108 mm (reproduced same size) Royal Photographic Society Collection

The gum bichromate process introduced in 1894 provided the photographer with a considerable amount of control over the final form of the print. The paper surface, image colour, overall and local strength of the image could all be controlled directly by the photographer. The print could be resensitised and reprinted any number of times to build up the image. Consequently gum bichromate prints vary widely in their appearance although the prints often resemble drawings in pastels, charcoals or crayons, lacking in fine definition.

Robert Demachy began to use the new process directly it became available and he became its best-known populariser internationally through exhibitions, articles and the book he published with Alfred Maskell, *Photo-Aquatint, or the Gum Bichromate Process* (1897). His prints were made with brown, grey and – as here – red ochre pigment. They were shown wherever photography was proclaimed as an Art medium, notably at the Photo-Club de Paris, The Linked Ring in London and the Photo Secession Galleries founded by Alfred Stieglitz in New York. Even so ardent a defender of 'straight' photography as Frederick H. Evans found much to admire in Demachy's work and proudly confessed that he owned 'two of M. Demachy's choicest examples. I know both are due in their finest values to hand control, but this is not apparent, or distractingly evident; their every inch tells me they are photographic; does that give me any shame concerning them? Rather does it add to their triumph in my eyes'. The process continued to interest avant-garde photographers up to about 1914, the year Demachy abandoned photography, but persisted in camera clubs for another generation and is still revived.

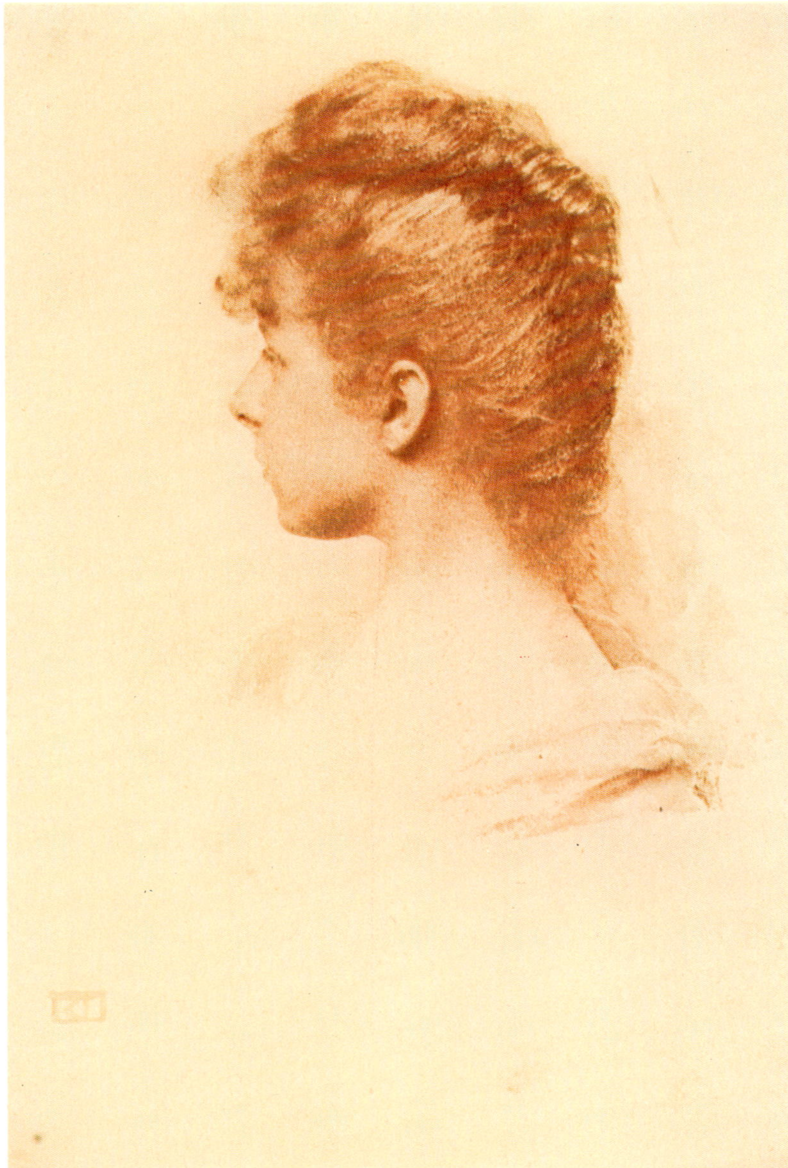

PLATE

33

Paul Martin British 1864–1942
A group of snapshots 1890s
Carbon prints in different colours (reproduced same size) Given by Mr E.V. Martin

Amateur photographers liked the carbon process for the degree of control over the final image it afforded as the carbon tissue could be transferred to any paper, or indeed other, surface. Carbon prints on rough papers, especially suited to the impressionistic photography of the 1890s, were popular for exhibition work. Just over a third of the prints exhibited at the Royal Photographic Society in the 1890s were made by the carbon process. The prints could be made in a very wide range of colours. The Autotype Company offered some 30-odd different colour-ways including Campari pink. Purists preferred the sobriety of grey and sepia but some photographers, like Paul Martin, experimented with a range of colours which reinforced the general atmosphere of their subject matter. Carbon printing was done by contact; small negatives gave small prints. To make large prints, large original or enlarged duplicate negatives had to be made.

Paul Martin habitually recorded his holidays in the 1890s, usually preserving the results in small albums. He printed mostly in platinum but also used carbon. The snapshots (the word Martin himself used) here were taken on holidays in Hastings (1893), Jersey (1896) and elsewhere. The albums show that he worked methodically with the same ingredients, here notably sea, beach and sky and their fluctuating light relations.

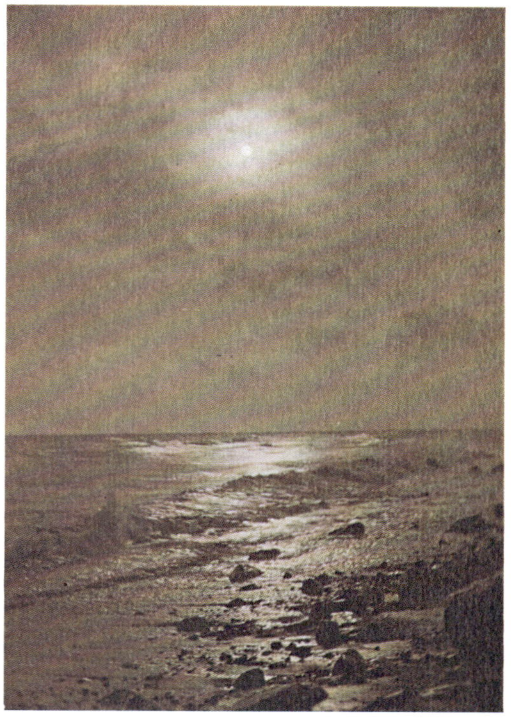
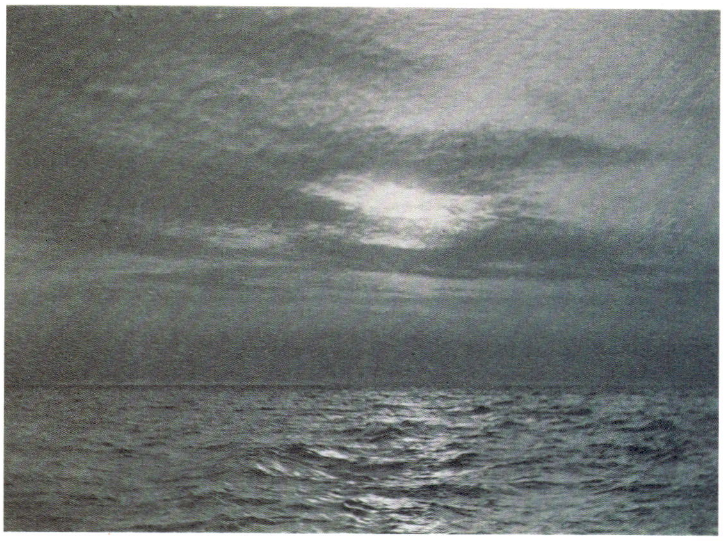
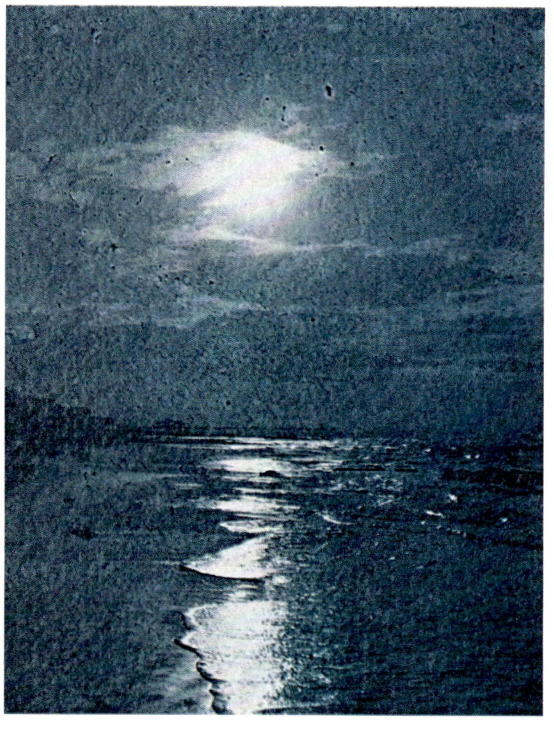
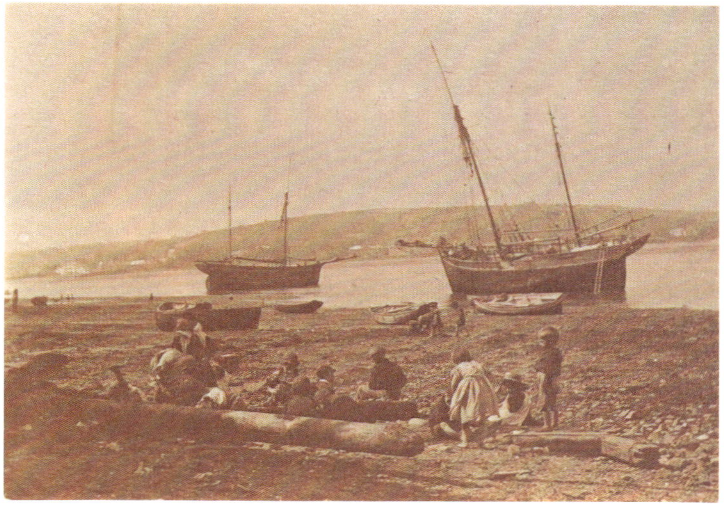

PLATE

34

Hippolyte Fizeau French 1819–96
Man and boy 1840s
Print from etched Daguerreotype plate
(reproduced same size) The Kodak Museum

William Henry Fox Talbot British 1800–77
Grasses 1852
Photoglyphic print
76 × 110 mm (reproduced same size) The Kodak Museum

William Henry Fox Talbot British 1800–77
The Congress of Deputies, Madrid 1858
Photoglyphic print
(reproduced same size) The Kodak Museum

One of the aims of many early experimenters in photography was to find a way to produce a printing plate directly from life without the need to make engravings or woodcuts. In the early 1840s Fizeau developed a process in which a Daguerreotype plate was etched with a solution which left the image unaffected but removed silver from the ground. The etched plate was electroplated with copper to make a more durable printing plate, which could be inked and printed many hundreds of times. Some small use was made of the process in the 1840s but it had disadvantages which limited its application. The foundations of successful photo-engraving were laid by Talbot in his patent of 1852. He suggested that a steel plate could be coated with a mixture of gelatin and potassium bichromate, which hardened when exposed to light. After exposure under a negative the unhardened gelatin was washed from the plate which was then etched with a suitable chemical. This penetrated the hardened gelatin only very slowly but attacked the exposed metal quickly. The etched plate could then be inked and printed. Talbot observed that while this method was suitable for fine lines it was less effective for broad areas of tone. He proposed that crossed gauze sheets be used to break the image up into fine lines which would retain the ink. This principle has been applied in photomechanical printing ever since. The photogram of grasses used the 1852 process. In 1858 Talbot patented an improved method in which the plate was not washed but coated with a powdered resin, set on the surface by heating. This technique, similar to a method used in aquatint engraving, broke up the image into minute ink-retaining areas, after etching with ferric chloride solution. His photoglyphic engraving process was entirely practical and formed the basis for the development of photogravure printing. Samples of Talbot's process were published in *Photographic News* in 1858 as reproductions of photographs of Spain, France and elsewhere by Soulier and Clouzard.

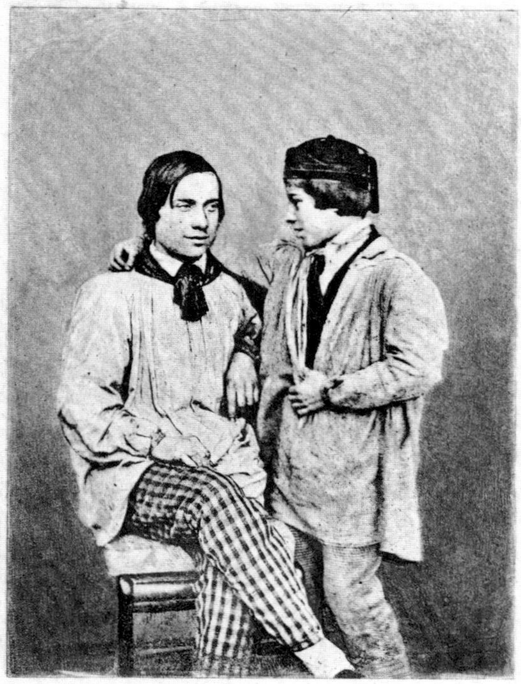

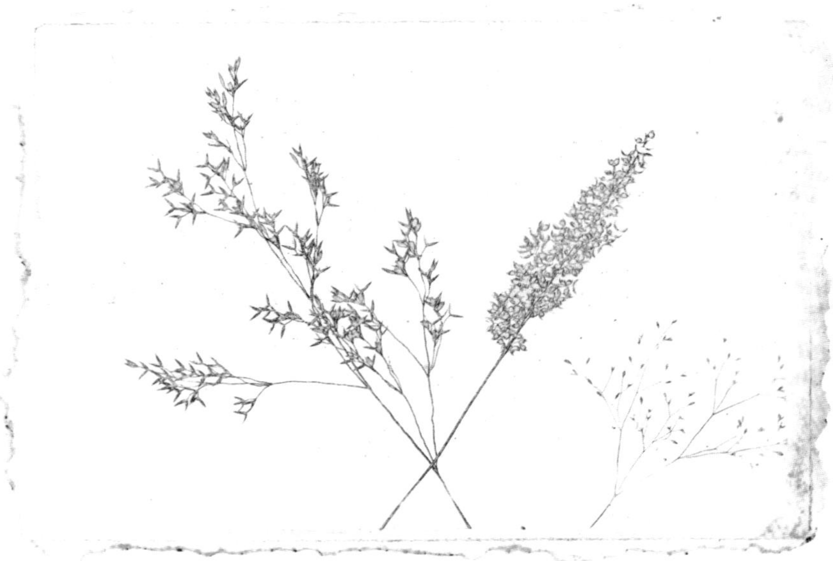

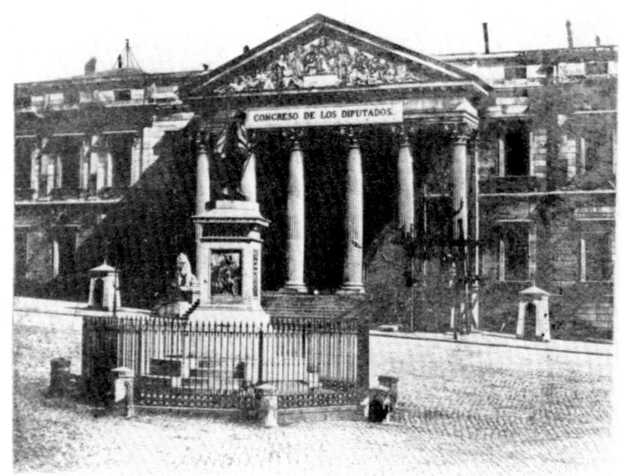

Photoglyph. ...... Presented with the "Photographic News."

CONGRESS OF DEPUTIES.

Madrid

PLATE

35

Peter Henry Emerson American, worked in Britain 1856–1936
In the Barley Harvest, Suffolk Published 1888
Photogravure
237 × 243 mm Mus. no. 2117–1896 Given by the photographer

Photogravure printing in the improved form developed by Karel Klič came into use around 1880 and was the first widely used photo-mechanical printing process (excluding Woodburytype) adequately to reproduce the half-tones of a photograph. Rather cheaper than carbon printing or Woodburytypes for quantity production, photogravure allowed prints of good quality to be run off quickly and at relatively low cost. The largest commercial use of the process was in art-publishing – the printing of facsimile copies of paintings (often coloured). Their grain structure, which can be seen with the naked eye, distinguishes them from true photographic prints.

This example first appeared in Emerson's handsome (20 × 16 inches) book *Pictures of East Anglian Life* (1888) (Plate VI). Afterwards Emerson made up portfolio sets of 10 prints and presented them to every photographic society in the country – and to the Museum as well. They were part of his vigorous opposition to prevailing taste in art photography, represented by crude combination printing, glossy albumen papers, wholesale retouching and disregard for the aspect of natural conditions. His position, deriving from a study of contemporary art (notably Whistler and Millet), was published as *Naturalistic Photography* (1889). Here he states his preference for photogravure as the finest medium in which to present pure photography, exceeding even platinum. The range of tints available in printing inks, carefully matched with the appropriate paper, 'beats mezzotint out of the field in its subtlety and delicacy'. He schooled a number of photogravure companies into carrying out the completely unretouched results he required.

Pictures of East Anglian Life carried epigraphs from Millet and from Oliver Goldsmith – 'But a bold peasantry, their country's pride/When once destroyed can never be supplied' – and was dedicated to the painter T.F. Goodall. Emerson wrote with close observation:

> Here one man is honing his scythe, while another, his face streaming with perspiration, has taken off his hat with which to fan himself, and now stretches forth his hand to his mate, who, leaving his rake in the field, has brought the bottle of 'home-brewed' from which they will all quench their thirst. Through the hot day they will work under the boiling summer sun until 4.30, or 'fourses', as it is now locally called, its name formerly being 'beavers'.

His text attacks rapacious 'upstart' landlords but although a Liberal as a young man he described his politics as 'uncompromising Tory' and wrote that his political ideal was 'Bismarck "without the religion"'.

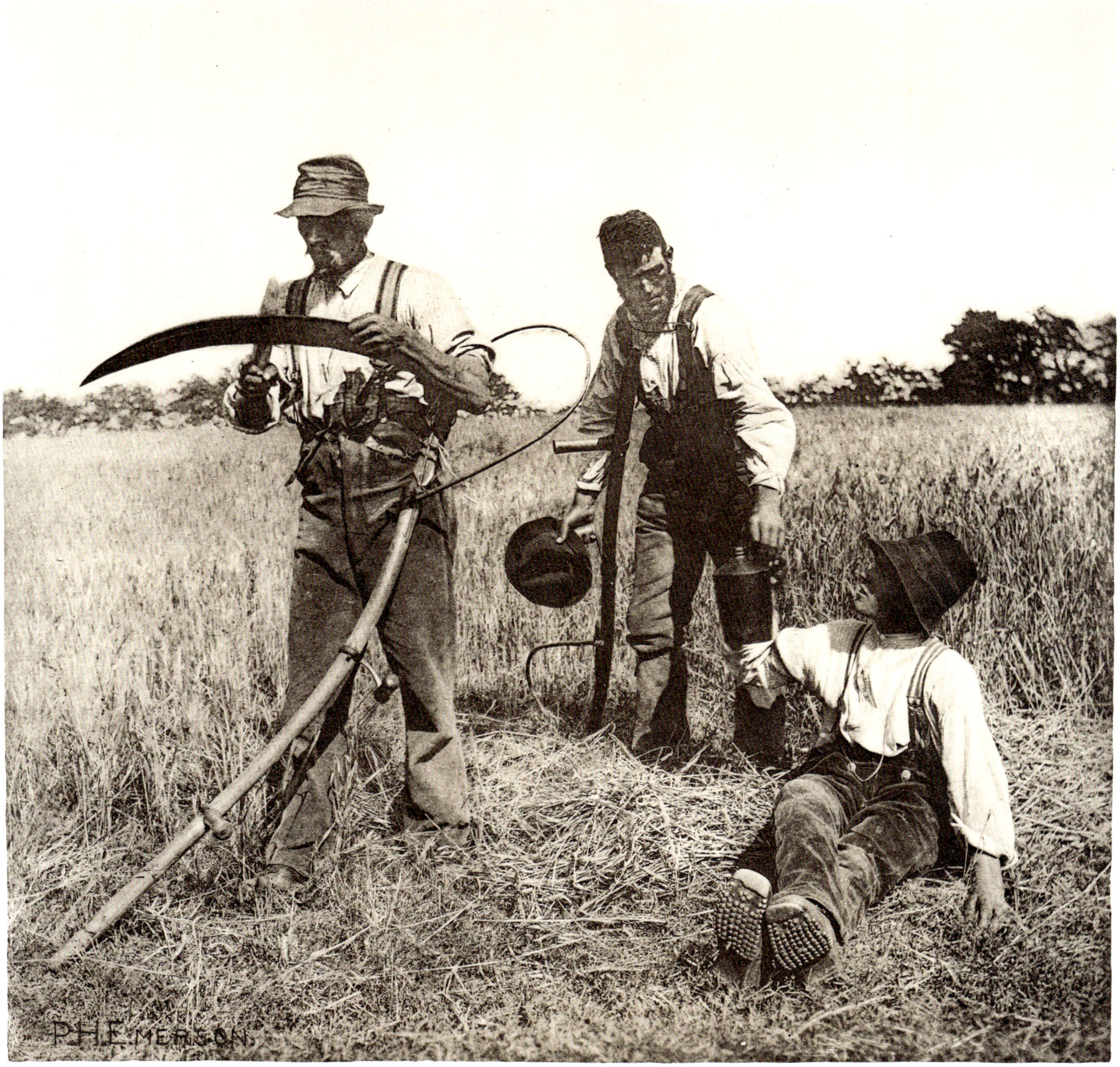
P.H.EMERSON.

PLATE

36

Alvin Langdon Coburn American, naturalised British 1882–1966
The Dragon 1903
Half-tone reproduction
138 × 177 mm (reproduced same size) Mus. no. Ph. 36–1981 Purchase

Half-tone reproduction, in which the image on a printing plate is broken up into a regular pattern of dots of different sizes, was not much used in its own right as an exhibition print-making method except during the experimental phase of the process about 1900. It was mainly used as a method of inexpensive mass reproduction of photographs which could be incorporated with text and printed on letter-press printing machines – unlike photogravure, where special presses were needed. It provided newspapers and magazines with an economic and practical method of illustration, and brought about the development of photo-journalism and press photography.

This example was published by Alfred Stieglitz in *Camera Work* for April 1904, together with other works by Coburn in photogravure. Coburn probably asked for his landscape photograph to be printed in green. The serpentine river in the plain is at Ipswich, Massachusetts. Coburn attended a summer school there given by the artist Arthur Wesley Dow in 1903. Through his own wood-block prints and writings Dow became a major channel for the flow of Japanese and Chinese pictorial methods into American art. He too made a print of the river, emphasising its decorative coils by placing the horizon high in the picture. The title Coburn gave his photograph is characteristic of his notions about landscape as the site of mythological forces – here implying a Far Eastern source and underlined, as it were, by the colour of the printing ink.

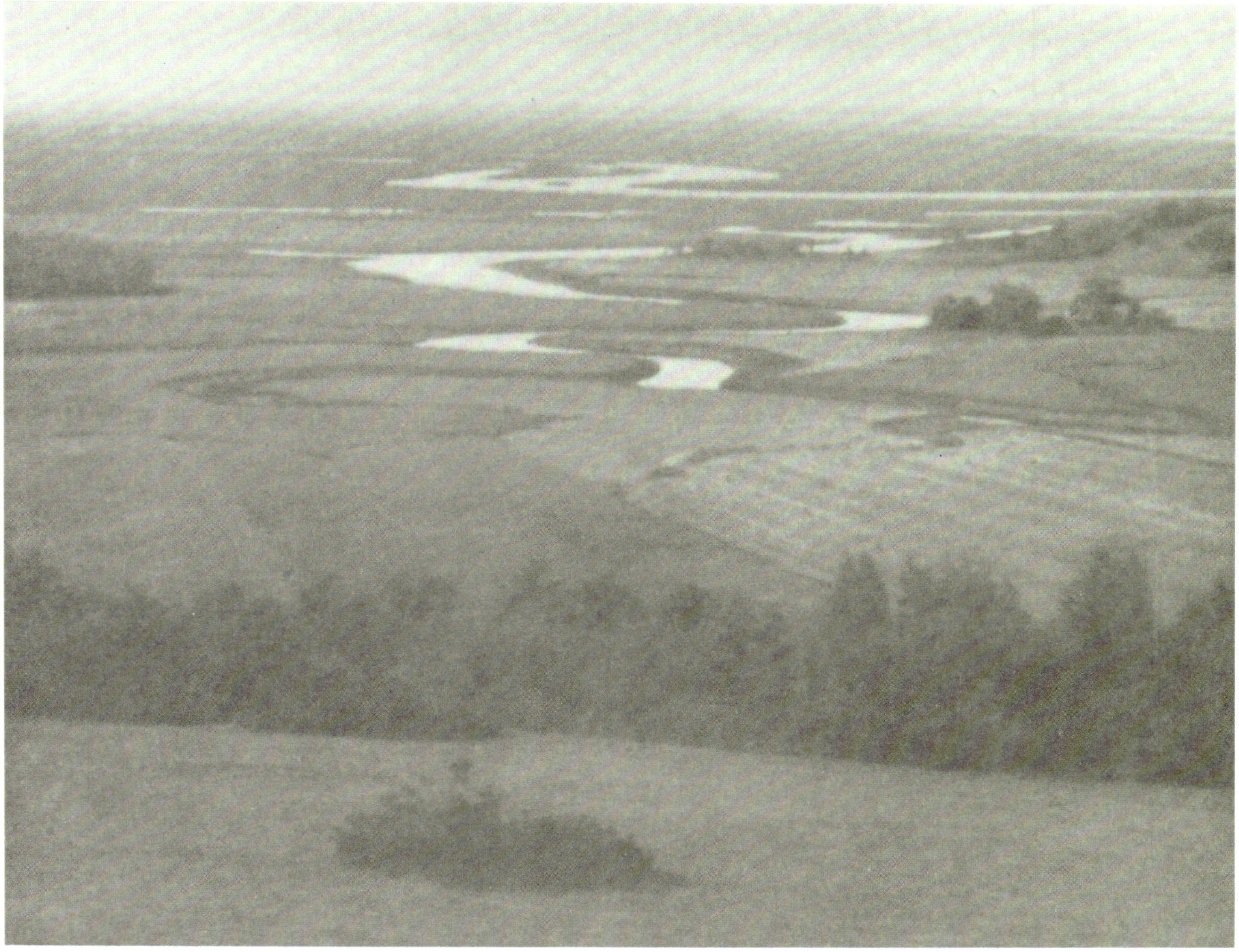

PLATE

37

The Dome of the Rock, Jerusalem Probably 1880s
Photochrom
165 × 224 mm Mus. no. 1068–1918 Given by Col. Willoughby Wallace C.M.G.

A modified form of Vidal's process (see PLATE 29) was the basis of the production of Photochrom prints. These were marketed widely in the late 1880s, 1890s and 1900s and were collected, as in this case, by travellers of antiquarian persuasions. At first sight resembling true colour photographs, they can be distinguished by the mechanical nature of the printing, seen when the print is examined with a magnifier. There is also the characteristic caption in gold lettering along the base of the print, with a serial number and 'P.Z.' – for Photochrom, Zurich.

This example is from a group of 800 photographs collected by Canon Wallace of Bristol in the 1870s and 1880s. His collection included photographs of drawings of the cathedrals of England and Wales, of modern buildings like the Eiffel Tower, together with views of the Swiss Alps and subjects of interest to tourists such as pigeons in Venice and a bullfight in San Sebastian.

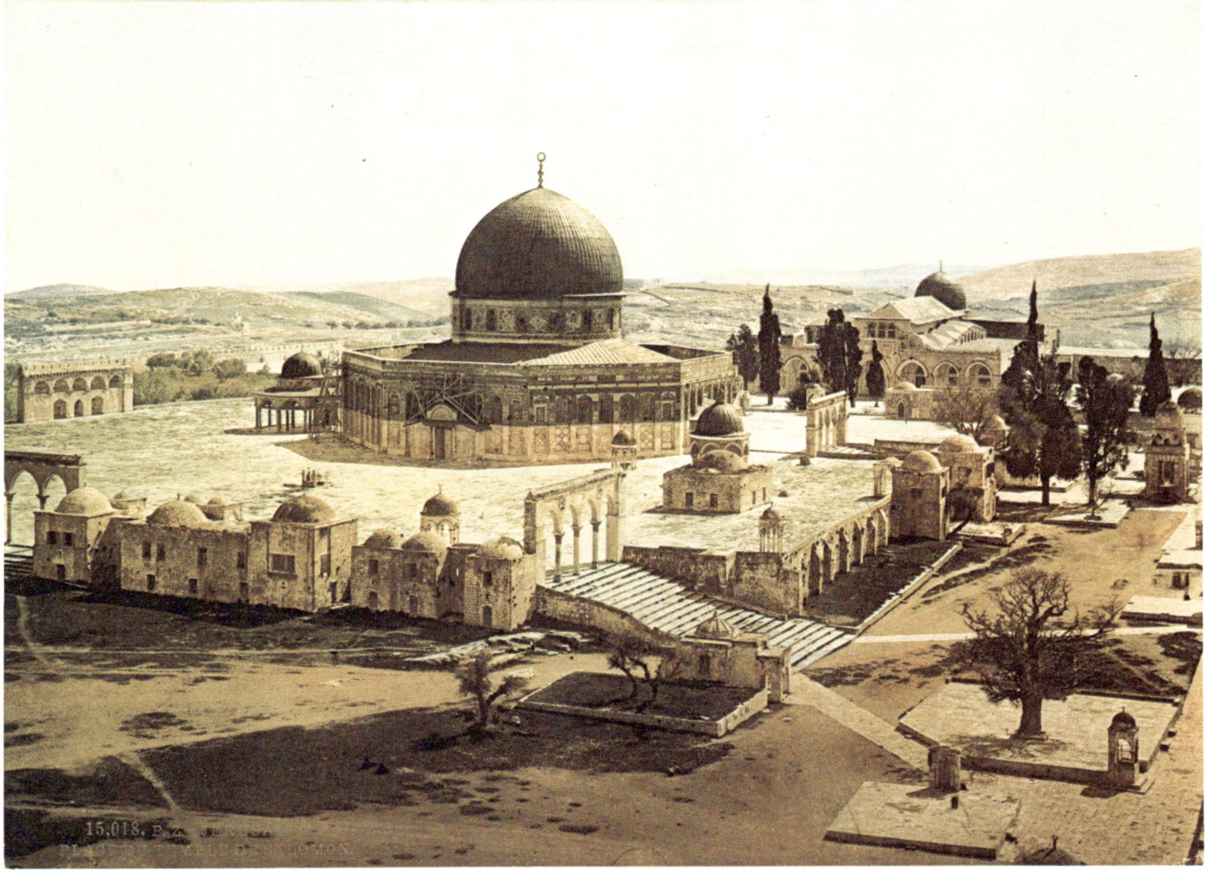
15,018.

FRONT COVER

Baron de Meyer German, worked England and USA 1868–1946
Tamara Karsavina (1885–1978) About 1908
Autochrome
89 × 119 mm Mus. no. 1234–1980 Purchase

The Lumière brothers announced the Autochrome process in 1904 but it was not marketed until 1907. Although not the first process for true colour photography it was the first to be widely and commercially available. It was based on a method of coating a glass plate with microscopic grains of potato starch dyed red, green and blue. This produced a random pattern of coloured dots on the plate, which was then coated with a gelatin-silver emulsion. This was exposed in the camera through the coloured mosaic: in good light for at least a second, often more. A reversal development process followed to produce a positive rather than a negative image and the result was a rather dense but usually accurately coloured transparency. The individual grains were microscopically small, but the random distribution tended to produce clumps of grains of the same colour, giving a coarser structure which could be visible to the naked eye – hence the 'Pointilliste' effect in some Autochromes. The Lumière Autochrome plates remained on the market until the 1930s.

The process was enthusiastically taken up by avant-garde photographers, notably Edward Steichen who used its late-Impressionist 'look' to record La Belle Epoque in sumptuous style. Baron de Meyer used the process for a very short period, perhaps only in 1907–09. In 1908 he writes to Alfred Stieglitz declaring that he is so taken with autochrome that black and white no longer satisfies him – but a year later abandons it in favour of black and white (in which medium he was a master printer). De Meyer and his wife were much associated with the ballet. This is one of a group of four autochromes taken for the Marchioness of Ripon, who first brought the Diaghilev Ballet to London in 1911, in the garden of Coombe, her house in Surrey (where Karsavina and Nijinsky danced for Queen Alexandra). De Meyer left London for New York in 1914 and became not merely a staff photographer for American *Vogue* but its first star photographer.

BACK COVER

Eva Watson-Schütze American 1867–1935
Woman admiring a print About 1910
Bromoil
203 × 156 mm Mus. no. Ph. 380–1982 Purchase

The Bromoil process, invented in 1907, is described in the Glossary. This example is by a member of the circle of Alfred Stieglitz, who collected examples of her work and published her photographs in *Camera Work*. She was a member of The Linked Ring and of the Photo-Secession. This example is signed with her monogram which echoes the calligraphic inscriptions typical of Chinese and Japanese prints and brush drawings (powerful inspirations for photographers of the period). The print being admired in the photograph is, however, likely to have been a fine photograph and this picture suggests the attention paid by photographers of the Stieglitz circle and in other international centres to the highest standards of craftsmanship in making photographic prints. Eva Watson-Schütze was praised by fellow-photographer and critic Joseph T. Keiley for the 'delicate taste and artistic originality' of her work.

THE CARE OF PHOTOGRAPHS

Elizabeth Martin

Conservation Department, Victoria and Albert Museum

The photograph consists of several components: the base, coating and image. The whole may be mounted on to a board with either an adhesive or a dry mounting tissue. All these layers have differing properties which react independently to the environment in which they are stored or displayed. The photograph can be protected from many harmful elements by virtue of commonsense.

Household enemies are: dust, which can scratch the surface; nicotine, which can stain; direct sunlight, which can embrittle, cause fading and deterioration; and moisture, such as condensation in bathrooms and kitchens, and damp in cellars, can encourage mould growth and can combine with excess processing chemicals and cause fading. The image should never be touched with fingers; oils, acids and chemicals in the skin can affect the surface, causing staining and irremovable finger-prints. Photographs should never be hung above radiators or open fires: they can become brittle, stains can ensue and fluctuating temperatures can encourage mould growth. Very dry and warm conditions can encourage insects such as silverfish and woodworm to attack the photograph in order to feed on the adhesives or wood used in the mounting, hingeing or framing of the object. Pressure-sensitive tapes such as Sellotape or masking tape should never be used even as first-aid measures for tears or hingeing: they become brittle and the residual adesive not only stains but is extremely difficult to remove. Fresh paint on walls, woodwork or furniture may emit peroxides which can be harmful to the photograph; photographs should therefore be stored in another room for at least two weeks.

Research into the case and conservation of the photograph is still in its infancy, but the life of the valued photograph can be extended by commonsense. Ideally, it needs to be mounted, hinged and stored in chemically inert materials. It has been discovered that one of the main destructive elements in mounting or storage materials is reducible sulphur. This causes silver in the image to tarnish; therefore anything used in connection with mounting or storage should be free of reducible sulphur. If photographs are to be displayed, they should be window-mounted in acid-free 100% ragboard (suppliers listed below) with glass to protect and preferably a metal frame. Ideally wooden backings should only be used if well isolated from the object. If left unframed, polyester sheeting can be used under the window of the mount to protect the surface; if unmounted, polyester sleeves (suppliers below) can be used to store the prints. Fragile photographs need a board to support them in the sleeve.

Albums with PVC sleeves are not recommended for long-term storage. Photographs should be kept away from sulphur-containing materials like brown paper, newspaper, old cardboard boxes.

Not all photographs have a paper base. Daguerreotypes and collodion positives ('Ambrotypes' in popular usage) which are usually cased, should be kept in a cool, dry and evenly temperatured environment; glass negatives or positives should be stored vertically in separate 'permalife' envelopes (suppliers below). If stacked, the weight of a pile may cause unnecessary breakages.

Neither broken or damaged photographs nor family albums have been discussed here. For the most part, any treatment needs expert advice. There are certain courses of action which are detrimental: Daguerreotypes should never be cleaned with 'silver dip'. Many recommended treatments become lethal, as often the true nature of the photograph constituents are not fully known (i.e. improper processing or chemicals used in development); if followed by a recommended, standard treatment, they can result in total loss of image. Many formulae are directed at either the base *or* the silver content of the image: this may result in damage to one or other.

Suggested Reading

The books and articles recommended below all provide practical advice on the handling, storage, identification and care of photographs.

T.J. Collings & F.J. Young, 'Improvements in some tests and techniques in photograph conservation', *Studies in conservation 21*, 1976, pp. 79–84.

S. Rempel, 'The care of black & white photographic collections: Identification of processes', *Technical Bulletin No.6*, Canadian Conservation Institute, November 1979.

S. Rempel, 'Care of black & white photographic collections: cleaning & stabilization', *Technical Bulletin No.9*, Canadian Conservation Institute, Ottawa, 1980.

A. Swan, 'The care and conservation of photographic material', '*Crafts Council*, London, 1981.

R.A. Weinstein & L. Booth, 'Collection, use and care of historical photographs', *American Association for state and local history*, Nashville, Tennessee, 1977.

Eastman Kodak Company, Rochester, N.Y., *Preservation of Photographs* (Kodak Publication No.F-30), 1979.

Suppliers

Secol Ltd, Kelvin Place, Thetford, Norfolk IP24 3RR. *For polyester sheets and sleeves.*

Conservation Resources (UK) Ltd, 33–35 Markham Street, Chelsea Green, London SW3 3NR. *For acid-free 100% ragboard, polyester sheets and sleeves and 'permalife' envelopes.*

Atlantis Paper Company, F3 Warehouse, New Crane Wharf, Garnet Street, London E1. *For acid-free 100% ragboard and archival materials.*

SELECT BIBLIOGRAPHY

Brian Coe's key and glossary have been formed over many years of examining photographs of all kinds and periods and wide reading in periodical literature so even an extensive bibliography would hardly be sufficient. This list covers the sources used in compiling the Commentary on the plates. Users of the book who wish to date portrait photographs which belong to a type employed over a long period of time (e.g. the albumen print) may find help in Madeleine Ginsburg's *Victorian Dress in Photographs* (Batsford, 1982). Especial mention should also be made of Helmut and Alison Gernsheim's panoramic and detailed *The History of Photography* (Thames and Hudson, 1969).

Another useful work is *Cassell's Cyclopaedia of Photography* edited by Bernard E. Jones, first published in 1911 and recently reissued by Arno Press. The same firm issued *Nonsilver Printing Processes: Four selections 1886–1927* edited by Peter C. Bunnell (New York, 1973). See also *The Albumen and Salted Paper Book: The History and Practice of Photographic Printing 1840–1895* by James M. Reilly (Light Impressions, 1980); and *The Keepers of Light: A History and Working Guide to Early Photographic Processes* by William Crawford (Morgan and Morgan, 1979). The following sources were useful and often essential in writing the Commentary section.

Beaumont Newhall, *The Daguerreotype in America*, New York, 1961

Beaumont Newhall, *The Pencil of Nature by W. H. F. Talbot 1844–46* (reprint, with introductory essay), New York, 1969

Isabelle Jammes, *Blanquart-Evrard et les Origines de l'Édition Photographique Française: Catalogue Raisonné des albums photographiques édités 1851–55*, Geneva and Paris, 1981

The Metropolitan Museum of Art, New York, *After Daguerre: Masterworks of French Photography (1848–1900) from the Bibliotheque Nationale* (catalogue by Bernard Marbot), New York and Paris, 1981.

National Portrait Gallery, *People in Camera 1839–1914* (catalogue by Colin Ford), London and Lucerne, 1979

Grand Palais des Champs Elysées, Paris, *L'Art en France sous le Second Empire* (catalogue of photography section by Eugenia P. Janis), Paris, 1979

Michael Millward and Brian Coe, *Victorian Townscape: The Work of Samuel Smith*, London, 1974

Valerie Lloyd, *Photography: the first eighty years*, Colnaghi & Co., London, 1976

Roy Flukinger, Larry Schaaf and Standish Meacham, *Paul Martin: Victorian Photographer* (Austin and London, 1977 and 1978)

Weston J. Naef, *The Collection of Alfred Stieglitz: Fifty Pioneers of Modern Photography*, New York, 1978

Walter and Naomi Rosenblum and Alan Trachtenberg, *America and Lewis Hine: Photographs 1904–1940*, Millerton, N.Y., 1977

Bruce Bernard, *The Sunday Times Book of Photodiscovery* (Notes on the Photographic Processes by Valerie Lloyd), London, 1980

BIBLIOGRAPHY

Cecil Beaton and Gail Buckland, *The Magic Image*, London, 1975

ed., Marianne Fulton Margolis, *Camera Work: A Pictorial Guide*, New York, 1978

Larry Schaaf, 'Anna Atkins' Cyanotypes: An Experiment in Photographic Publishing,' *History of Photography*, April, 1982

Musée Carnavalet, Paris, *Etienne Carjat 1828–1906: Photographe*, Paris, 1982

Charles Baudelaire, *Oeuvres Completes* (2 vols.), Paris, 1975

Enid Starkie, *Baudelaire*, London, 1957

Claude Pichois, *Iconographie de Baudelaire*, Paris, 1960

Lunn Gallery/Graphics International Ltd, *Photo-Secession* (catalogue by Peter Galassi), Washington, D.C., 1977

Stefan Lennert Gallery et al., *Heinrich Kühn* (texts by Elizabeth Pollock and Odette M. Appel-Heyne), Munich, 1981

Bill Jay, *Robert Demachy 1859–1936: Photographs and Essays*, London, 1974

Ian Jeffrey, *The Real Thing: An anthology of British Photographs 1840–1950*, Arts Council of Great Britain, London, 1974

Michael Weaver, *Alvin Langdon Coburn: Man of Mark*, the Royal Photographic Society, Bath, 1982